Introduction :

The question is often asked, Dr. Dunn, why do you do what you do?" I boldly say I had an awakening moment in my life while going through one of many storms. I am no longer submerged in my pain; God has equipped me with the ability to stand. I now embrace my life with no regrets. I have formed love and compassion for people and cleared my mindset completely. I choose to obey the mission at hand. God's power is real! The enemy has no power over my life. My mission is to learn, teach, motivate, inspire, and help restore brokenness. I am an all-rounder, a booster of encouragement, a motivator at hand when it comes to life skills. I can tell you everything you need to hear in a few words. I will support you and encourage you through prayer and positivity. I am coming through spreading the light in dark places, to set your torch on fire, to heal past pain and trauma, and to teach you how not to let your light go dim. However, to help you re-enter with the Father, the Son, and the Holy Ghost, to redirect peace, love, and joy all over you. Make peace the goal, freedom the objective, and God the processor. Remember, nothing happens overnight; it all counts as a work in progress. Now, walk with the favor that is over your life, re-entering with nothing but peace and a sound mind. With God, I can show you how to incorporate peace and praise to uplift your spirit man, to explore and experience breakthroughs like you have never done before, and learn how to love again with a whole heart and seek His will for your life, no matter your imperfections.

Dedication:

In the pages of this book, I dedicate my words to the journey of healing past pain and trauma. May it guide you towards keeping your light shining brightly and reconnecting with the Father, the Son, and the Holy Ghost. Thank you to my husband, family, and friends, for believing in me. I hope you let this be a source of redirection, flooding you with peace, love, and joy. Make peace your goal, freedom your objective, and let God be the processor of your transformation. God is clear and heartfelt; he gives off positive energy and help you redirect and feel positive emotions. Remember, nothing happens overnight; it's all a work in progress. Walk with the favor that is over your life, re-entering a realm of peace and a sound mind. With God's guidance, discover how to incorporate peace and praise to uplift your spirit. Explore and experience breakthroughs like never before, learning to love again with a whole heart and seeking His will for your life, imperfections, and all.

Table of Contents:

Chapter 1: Conqueror ……………………………………………………..5
Chapter 2: You are the Mission……………………………………………67
Chapter 3: Peace of Mind……………………………………………………123
Chapter 4: Healing from Within……………………………………………..166
Chapter 5: Trust Yourself………………………………………………….. 210

Chapter 1 : Conqueror

The beautiful spirit you have blesses and encounters everyone. Thank you for accepting the assignment. Everything you deserve is already yours. Don't let your thoughts overwhelm you; keep holding on. Take positive steps every day and embrace your solid ground. Little by little, day by day, and minute by minute, you are achieving your life goal. Growth and life-changing events are always scary, but you are brave. Life has so many different seasons, and we all go through them.

God has you covered.

You are indescribable in so many words. I pray that God continues to break seals that will release and pour out an overflow of blessings.

It is your time.

You are God's greatest joy.

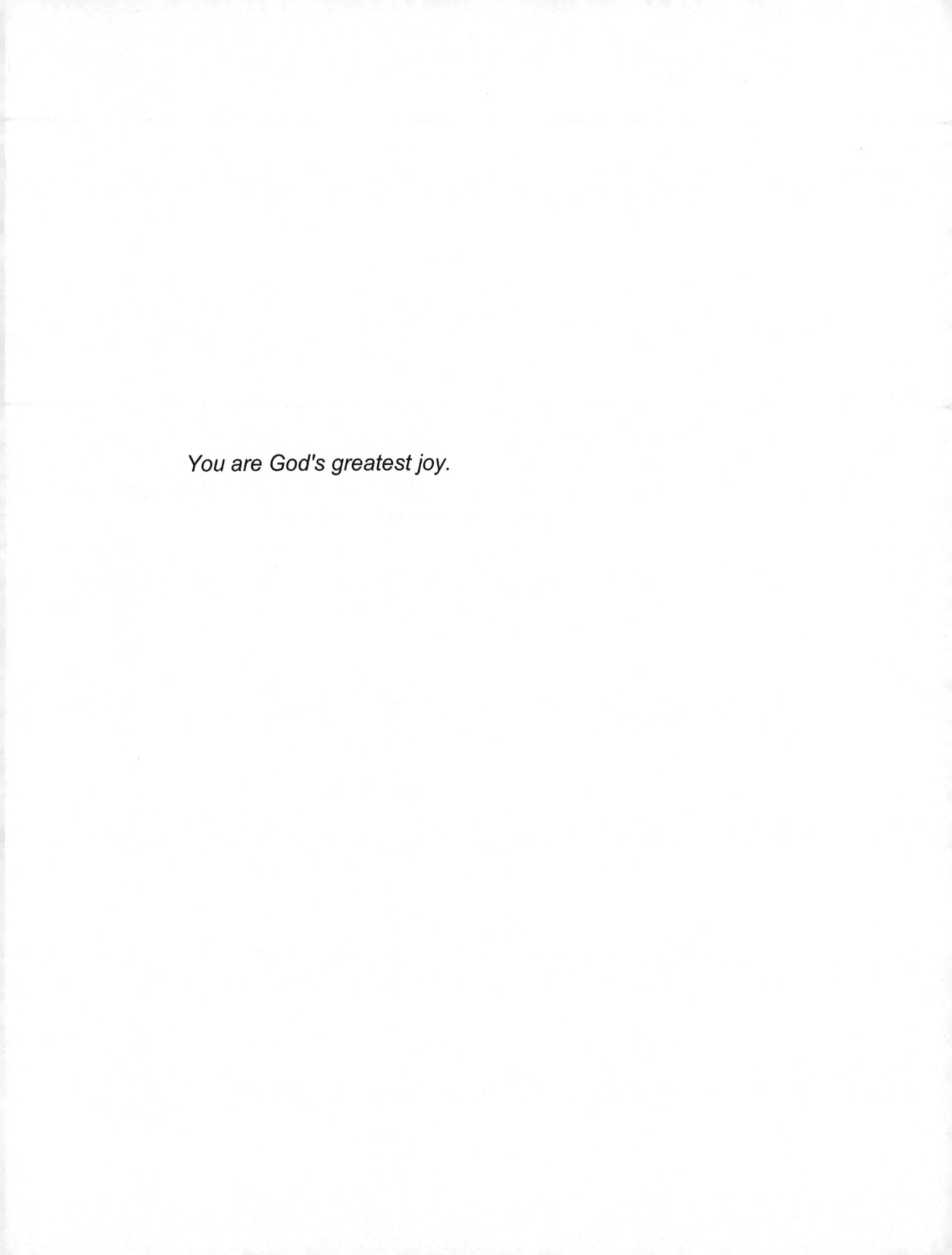

I am convinced that God can pull us out of anything, especially our thought process. Do not let your mind take you off focus.

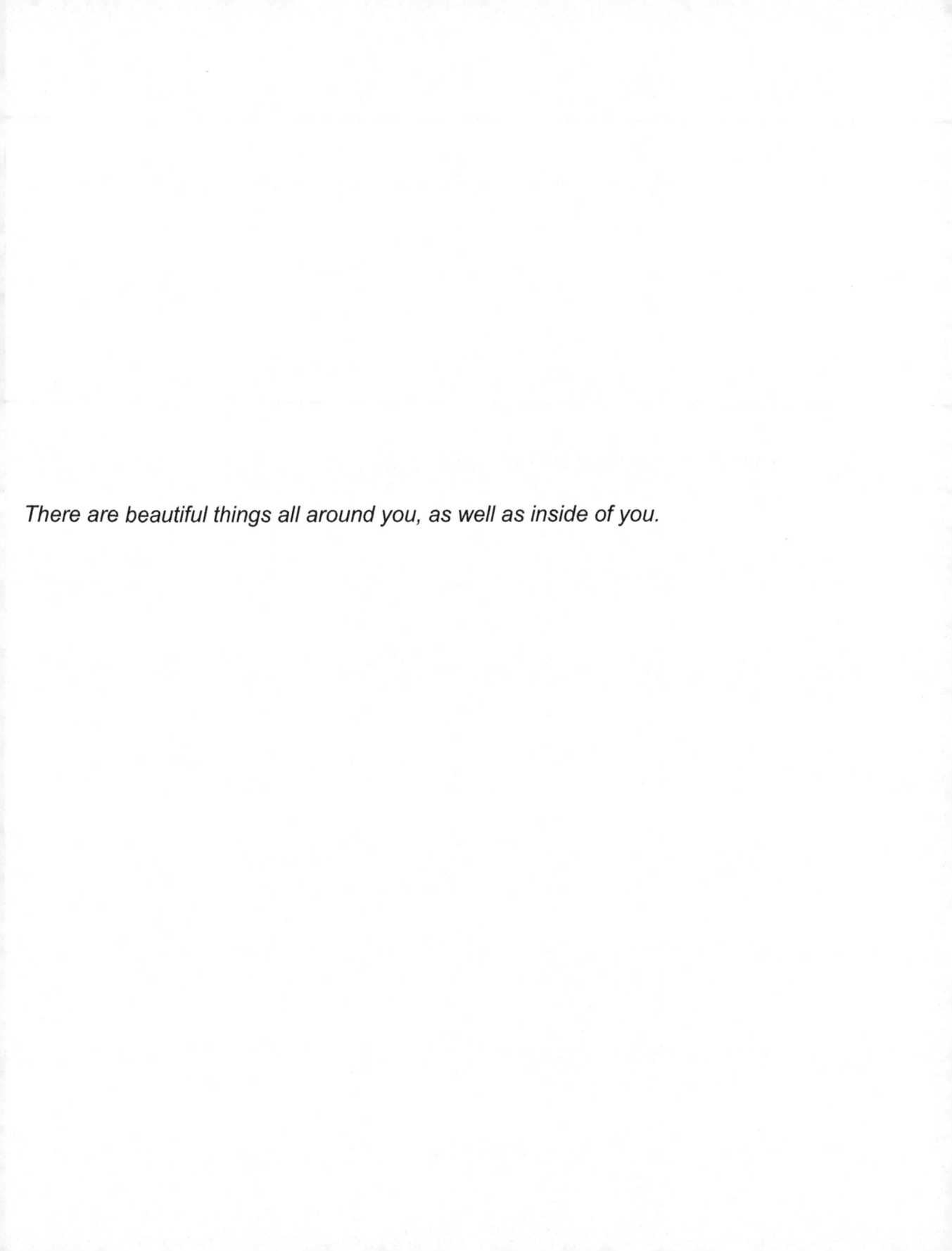

There are beautiful things all around you, as well as inside of you.

Your hidden talents are behind your smile.

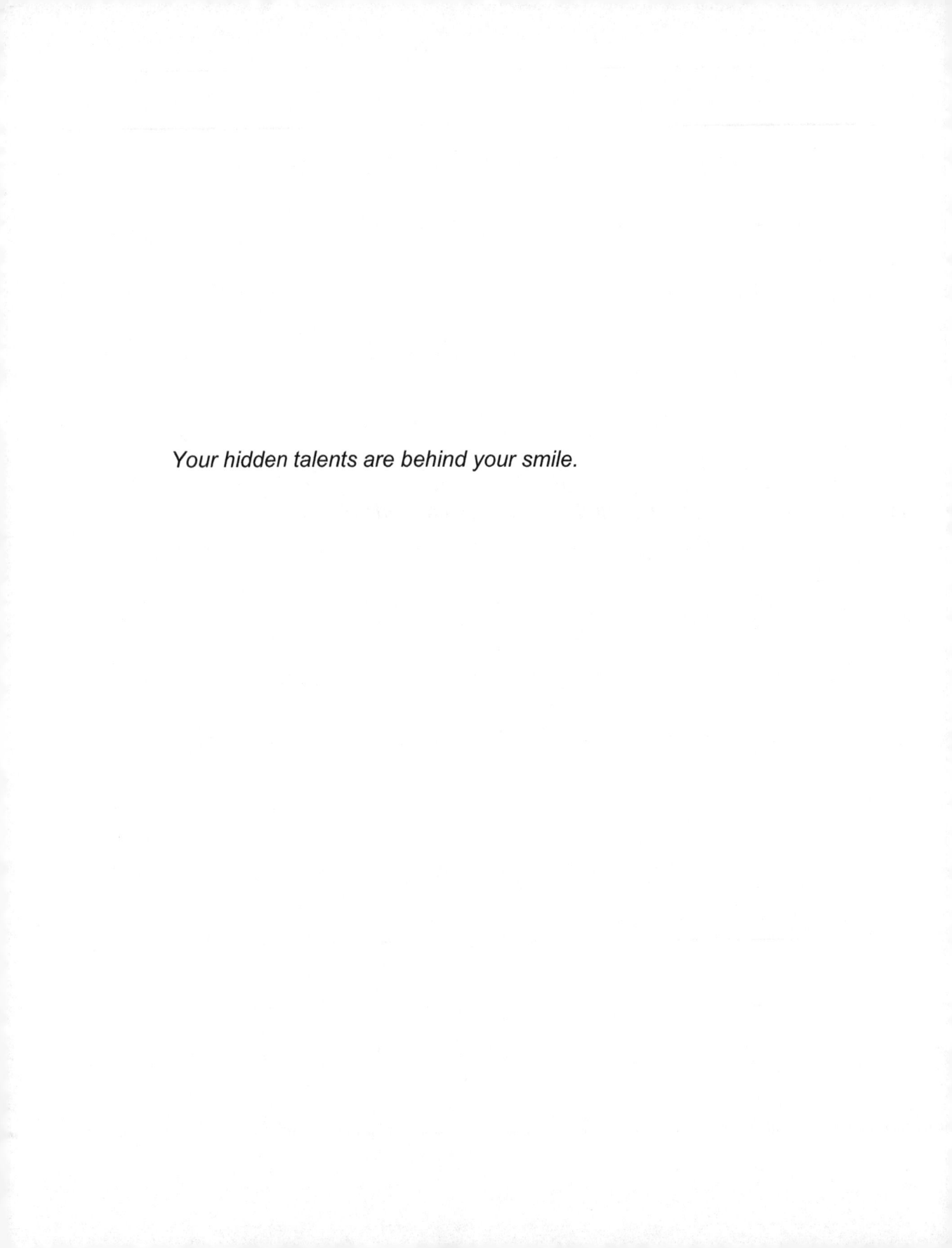

Absolutely! Always stay connected to a good place – wherever you find peace, joy, and happiness. Remember to release and expose yourself to good mental health; it will add balance to everything.

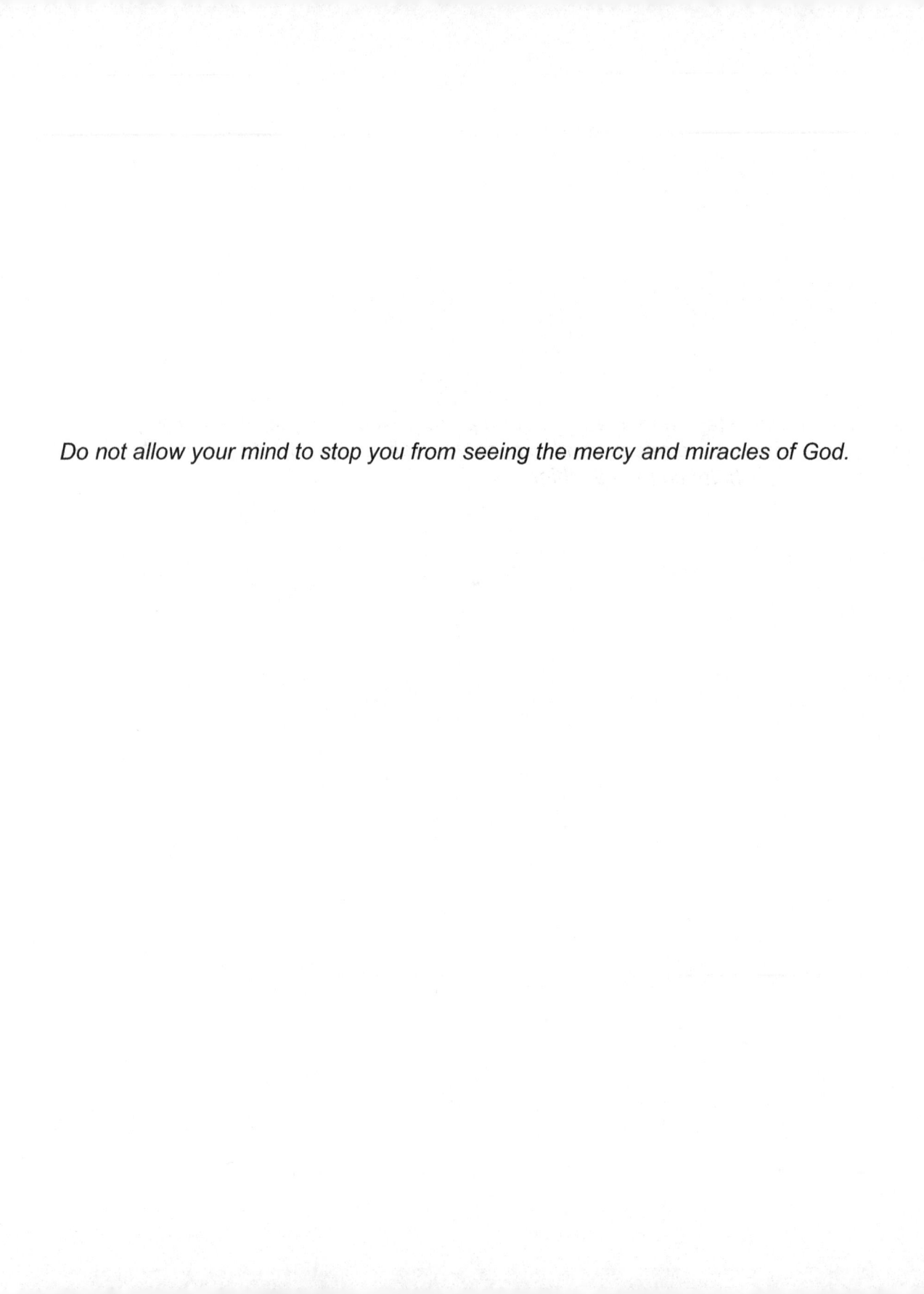

Do not allow your mind to stop you from seeing the mercy and miracles of God.

This is not the season to compare.

Don't rob yourself of your joy when God has opened plenty of doors because you are the chosen one. Don't just take my word; believe it and walk in it.

Know that God surrounds you with mercy and grace.

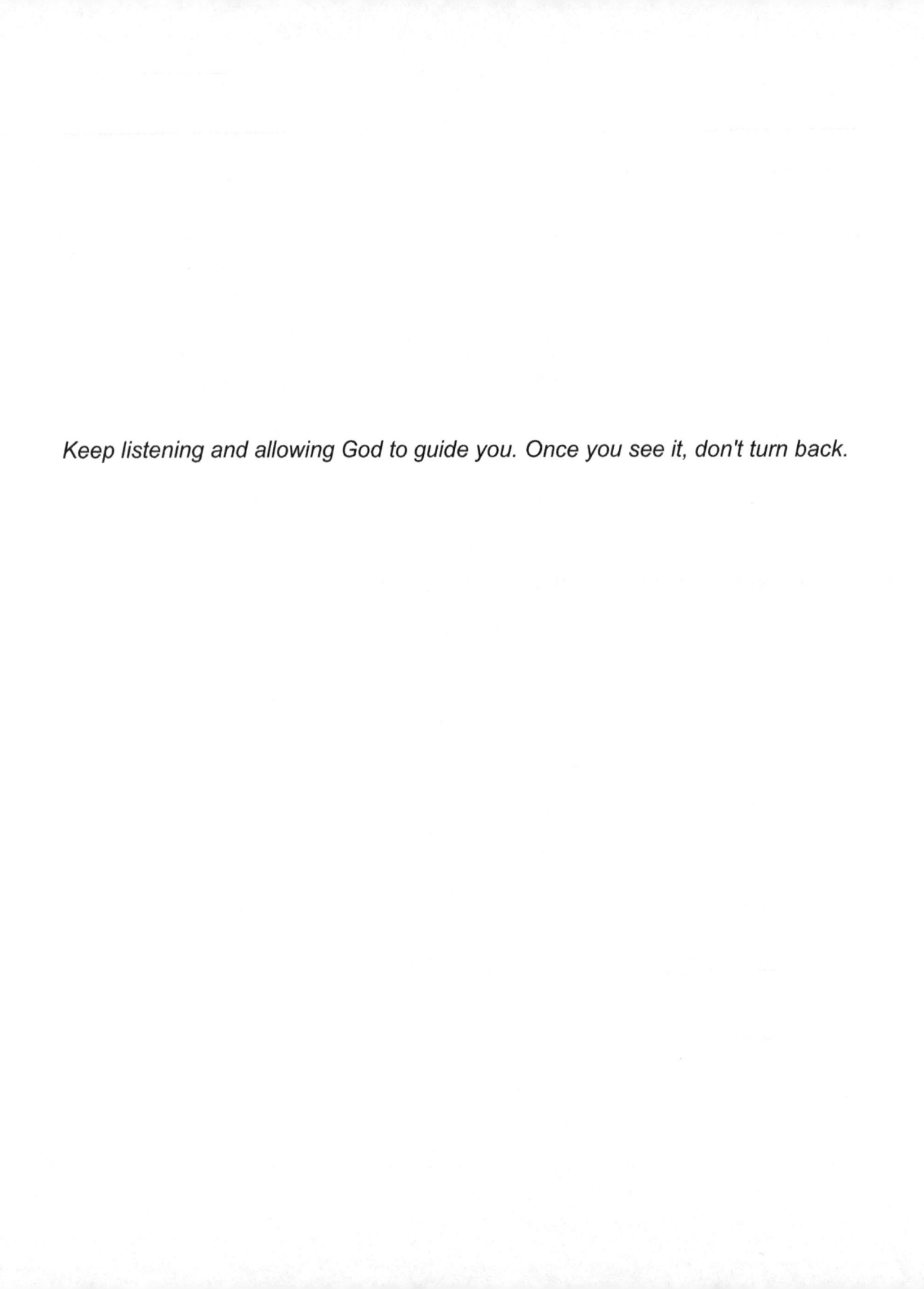

Keep listening and allowing God to guide you. Once you see it, don't turn back.

The person you are is wonderful.

God is working it out.

It will continue to get better and better.

Watch out for anxiety. If you feel it coming, just breathe—keep breathing. Ask anxiety to go, then let anxiety go. Tell anxiety it serves no purpose. Thank you, Lord.

Allow nothing or anyone to steal or rob you of your joy, not even yourself. The sabotaging days are over. Hallelujah!

I appreciate your gratitude. Keep being yourself. We've been through plenty of stages in life, and it's not over. Love the person you see in the mirror—the one you are right now is wonderful.

Embrace the person you are becoming and always find forgiveness in your heart. Love and encourage yourself.

Occasionally, your mind produces invisible walls. Trust me, they are up. Despite your mind denying their existence, various blockages like spiritual walls, mental walls, emotional walls, relationship walls, rejection walls, and more exist. It's essential to realize that it was your thinking trying to take control, but God.

The time is now to tear down your walls, piece by piece. Your mind will suggest that you overlook your mental thoughts because it does not want to be healed and cannot see the blockage that is there. We cannot see God with our natural eyes, but God is moving; it's all a process.

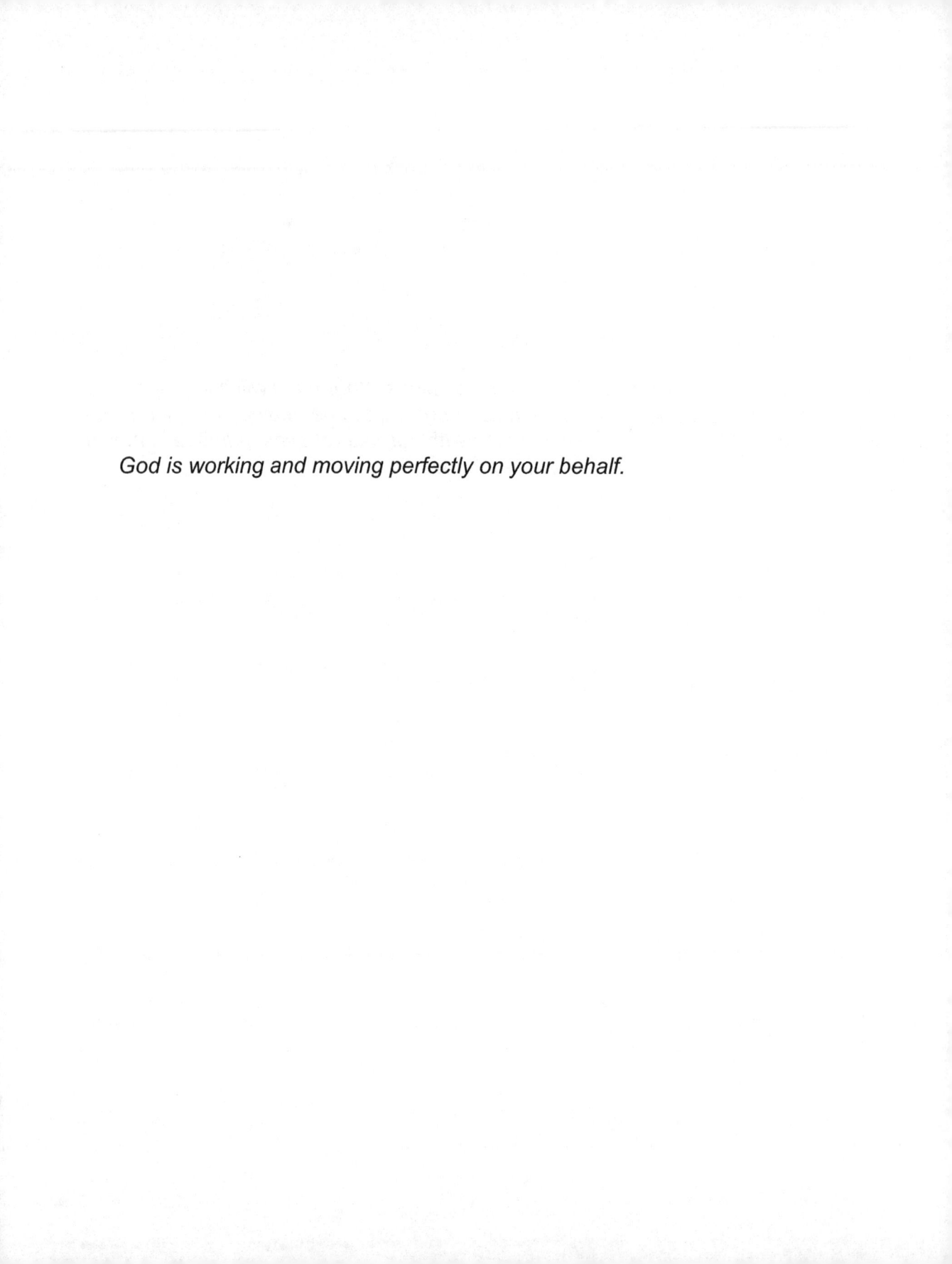

God is working and moving perfectly on your behalf.

Love the person you will be, and never stop walking in your joy.

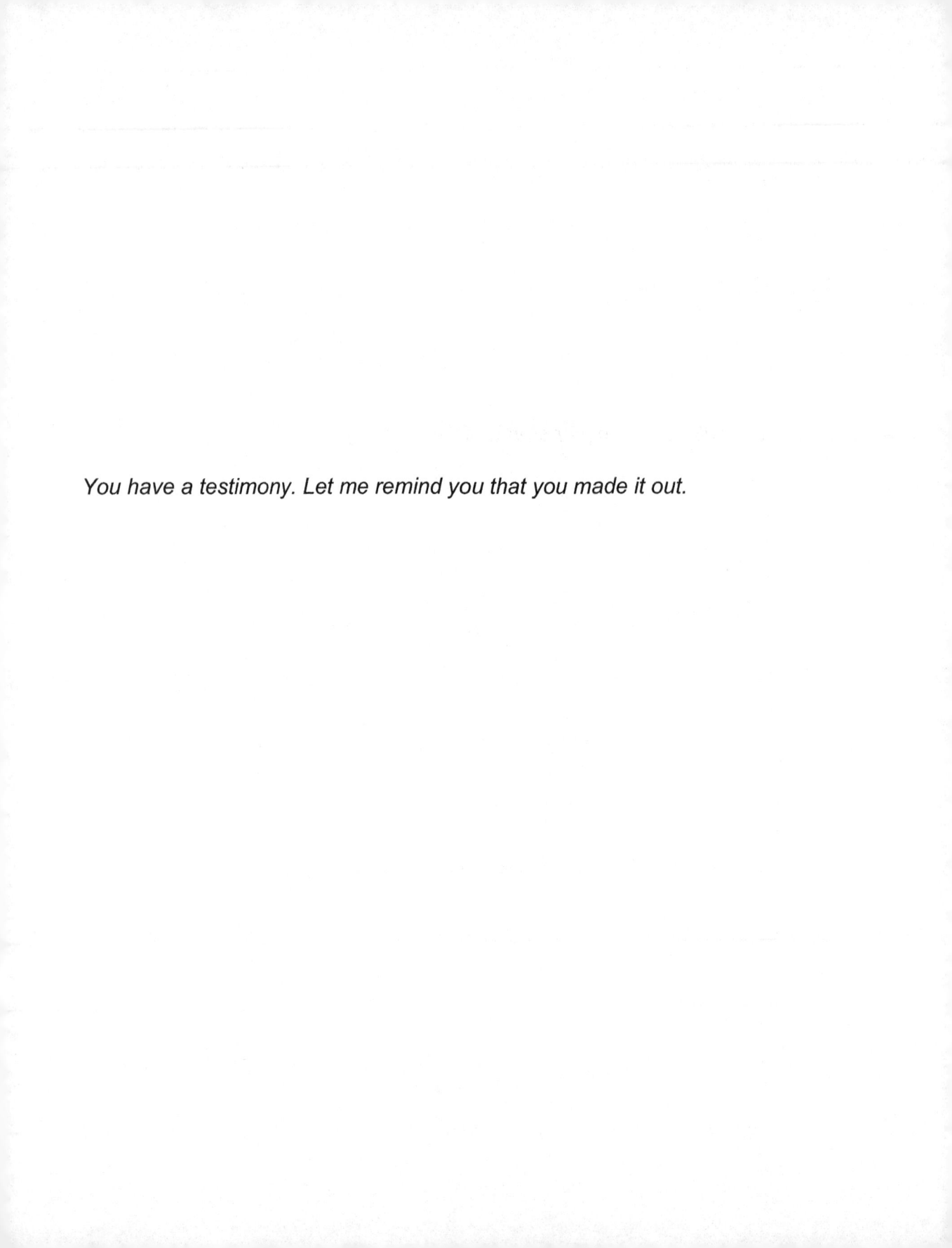

You have a testimony. Let me remind you that you made it out.

Keep elevating with your head held high. You are powerful right now.

Love the person you are becoming because the roles you are fulfilling are a destiny that releases pain and trauma.

Be amazed that God is wonderful.

Today is the day that I express gratitude for my life and yours. Lord, help me stand on your word. Now is the time for me to move, leaning on your word. Give me peace in my heart that stops the ringing in my head. Grant me love that fills the room with your spirit and removes fear from my hand. No more leaning to the right or the left. I am going to stand on your word, Lord. Thank you for giving me peace in my mind and love in my heart.

Lord, I ask you to store your word in my heart.

Remember that God has ordained every step you've taken, even if it seemed like a detour.

I appreciate kind words.

Changing your mindset for the better can release negative energy that has been holding you back.

God is guiding you towards blessings.

I'm proud to know you, happy to have you as a friend, a brother/sister.

Even in silence, dreams come true.

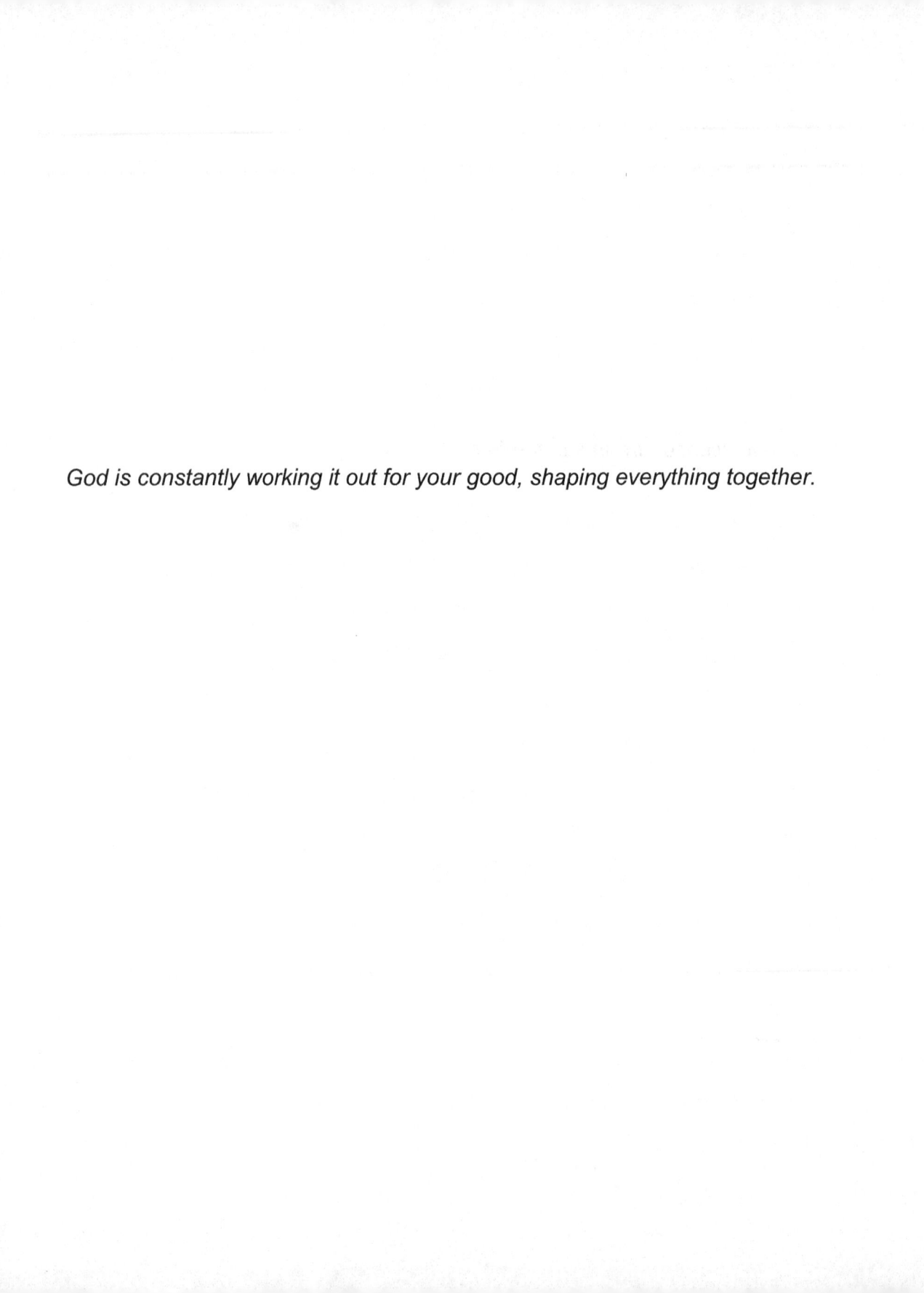

God is constantly working it out for your good, shaping everything together.

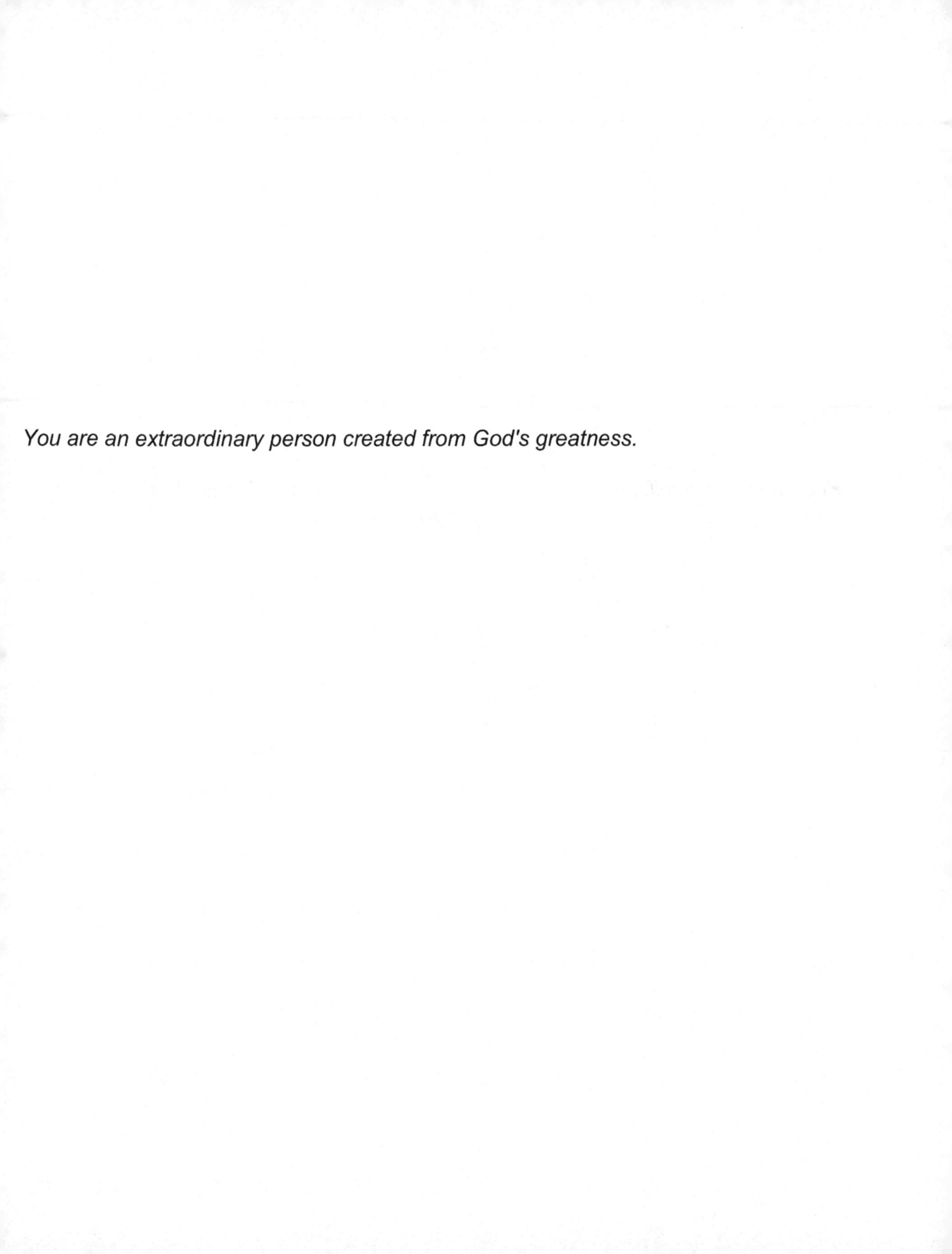

You are an extraordinary person created from God's greatness.

Keep being yourself, love those around you, and know that God is always present. Amen.

God first.

God has you in a special place in His heart, and that resonates in my heart as well. Your intuition is magical and powerful. God is growing you spiritually and upward. Keep moving in the direction that brings you peace because God said He is going to restore happiness and prosperity.

As human beings, we wake up with so much on our minds, spending a significant amount of time living in our heads. Work on uplifting yourself daily is crucial. We can't control life situations, but allowing the past to affect us can handicap and impact our everyday lives. If history awakens past trauma, it may connect to the future unless we cut it off. Don't let your mind choose to accept past pain. Adapt, listen, and remove the blinder then understanding your present feelings.

Take a moment to breathe and move forward, not backwards . Release the hold on tears, pain, and associated emotions. Step out of your comfort zone, allowing the past to be in the past, realizing it might be holding blessings back. Embrace the new day and walk in your newfound light.

It's natural to feel broken at times, but it could be that you're holding on to old pain that no longer serves you. While others have moved on, you may find yourself wallowing in the heat within yourself. To break free, acknowledge the greatness within you. If you sense something holding you back and conflicting messages about your greatness, consider seeking support from friends, family, or a professional to help navigate and overcome these feelings. Remember, your potential for greatness is real, and you can move beyond the limitations you feel.

A positive message! I'm here to help you navigate through the day. Stepping out of your comfort zone brings necessary growth, and God's guidance is invaluable through all storms.

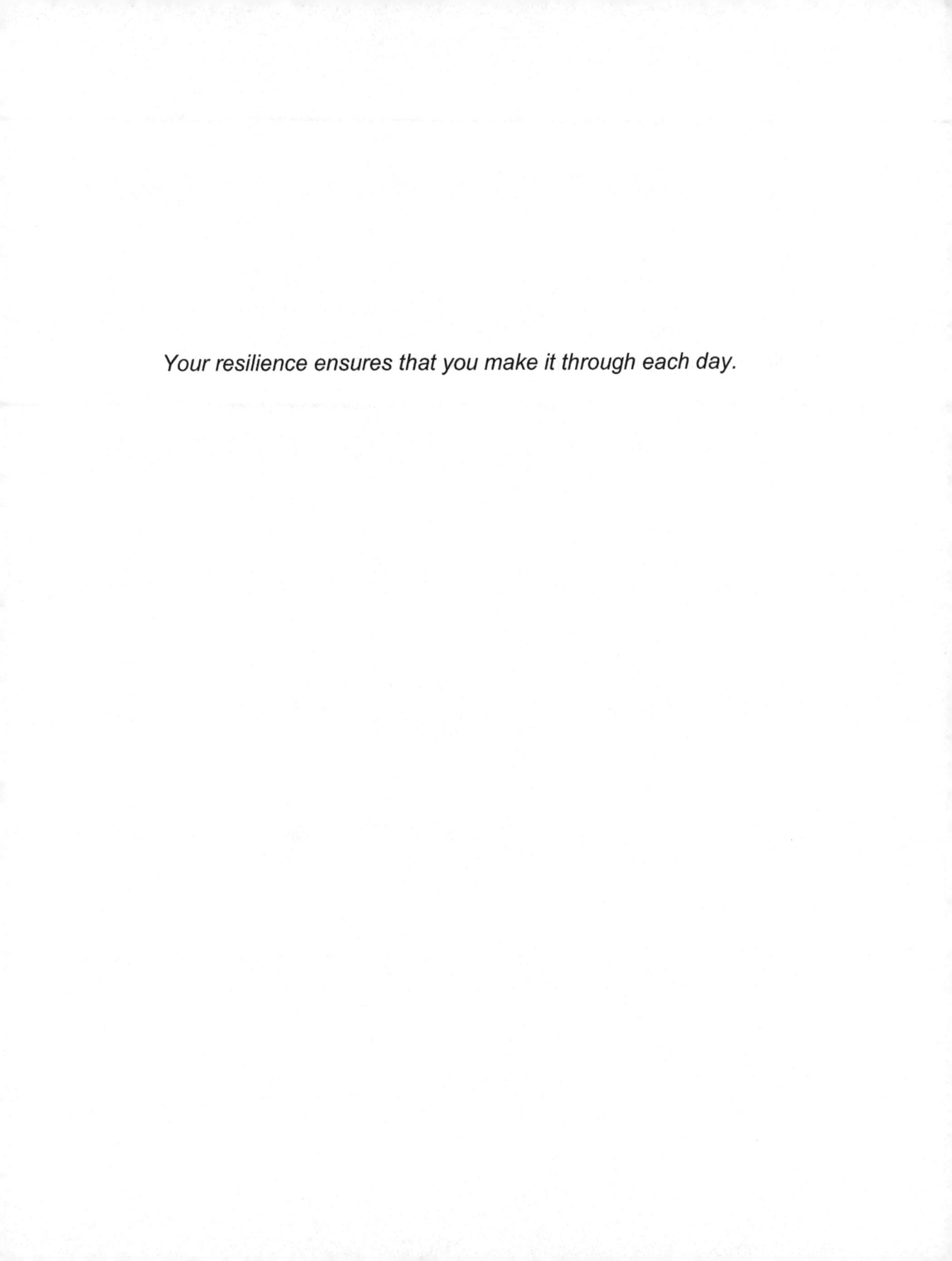

Your resilience ensures that you make it through each day.

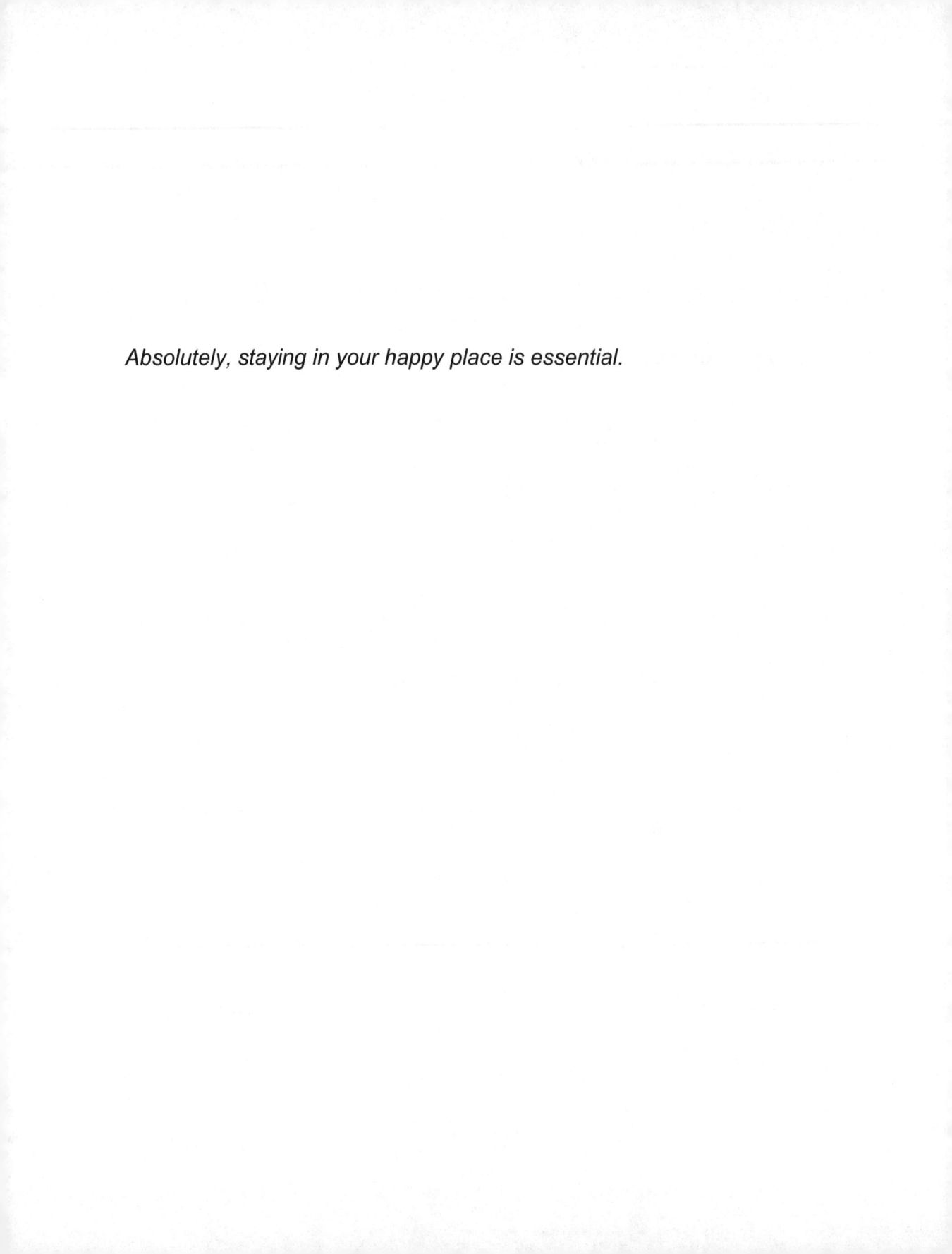

Absolutely, staying in your happy place is essential.

When you step out for the day, clear your thoughts. Get to a place where you can zone into God because negativity might be trying to become the predominant experience.

Prioritize maintaining a positive and joyful mindset.

It will provide a word that adds hope and a peace that surpasses all understanding, nourishing your body with the fullness and satisfaction that only God can add. On a positive note, seek God's presence.

Staying in your happy place is crucial.

Stay encouraged, regardless of the obstacles that come your way. Let peace surround your heart and mind at all times. You are perfectly made. Keep your focus positive and great. Allow happiness to overwhelm you. Let peace surround your heart emotionally, physically, and mentally.

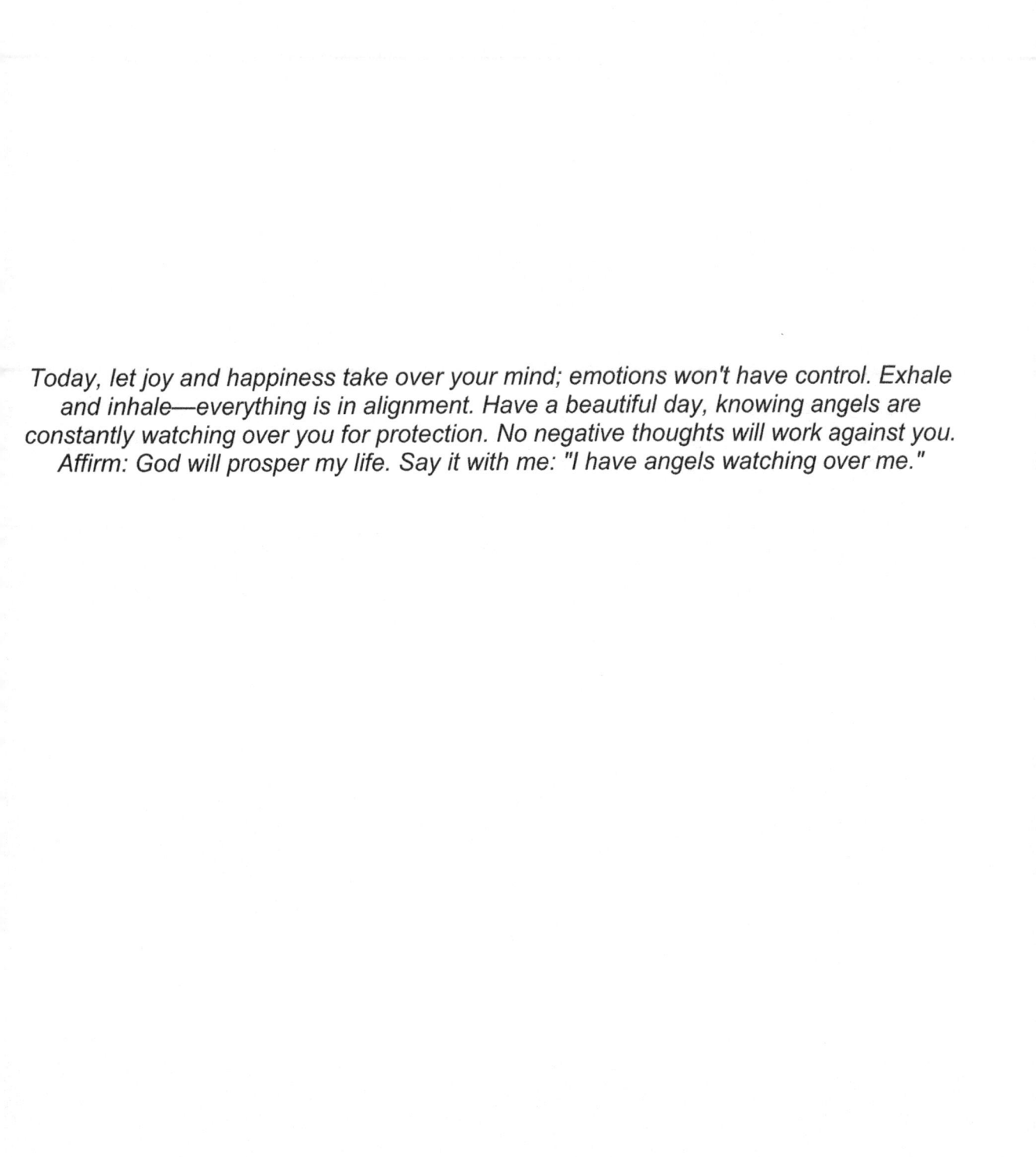

Today, let joy and happiness take over your mind; emotions won't have control. Exhale and inhale—everything is in alignment. Have a beautiful day, knowing angels are constantly watching over you for protection. No negative thoughts will work against you. Affirm: God will prosper my life. Say it with me: "I have angels watching over me."

Money is just a tool. Start to feel a little relief now. It's just a tool that will bring more money and resources than usual. Your good health and safe finances are on the horizon. Expect a large sum of money from somewhere soon. Still, no matter how secure your finances become, keep watching God.

Everything will be okay.

It is going to increase more and more because you look to Him. This is God's word: people will realize who you are when you know who you are. There is power in just being yourself. Occasionally, you must go find yourself; it is possible to get lost while being on the right path.

The pathway of life is constantly changing, and your patience will be put to the test. Be patient when things do not go as planned. Watch God move on your behalf in your life.

Get so concerned with the Lord that you wouldn't have time to entertain negative thoughts.

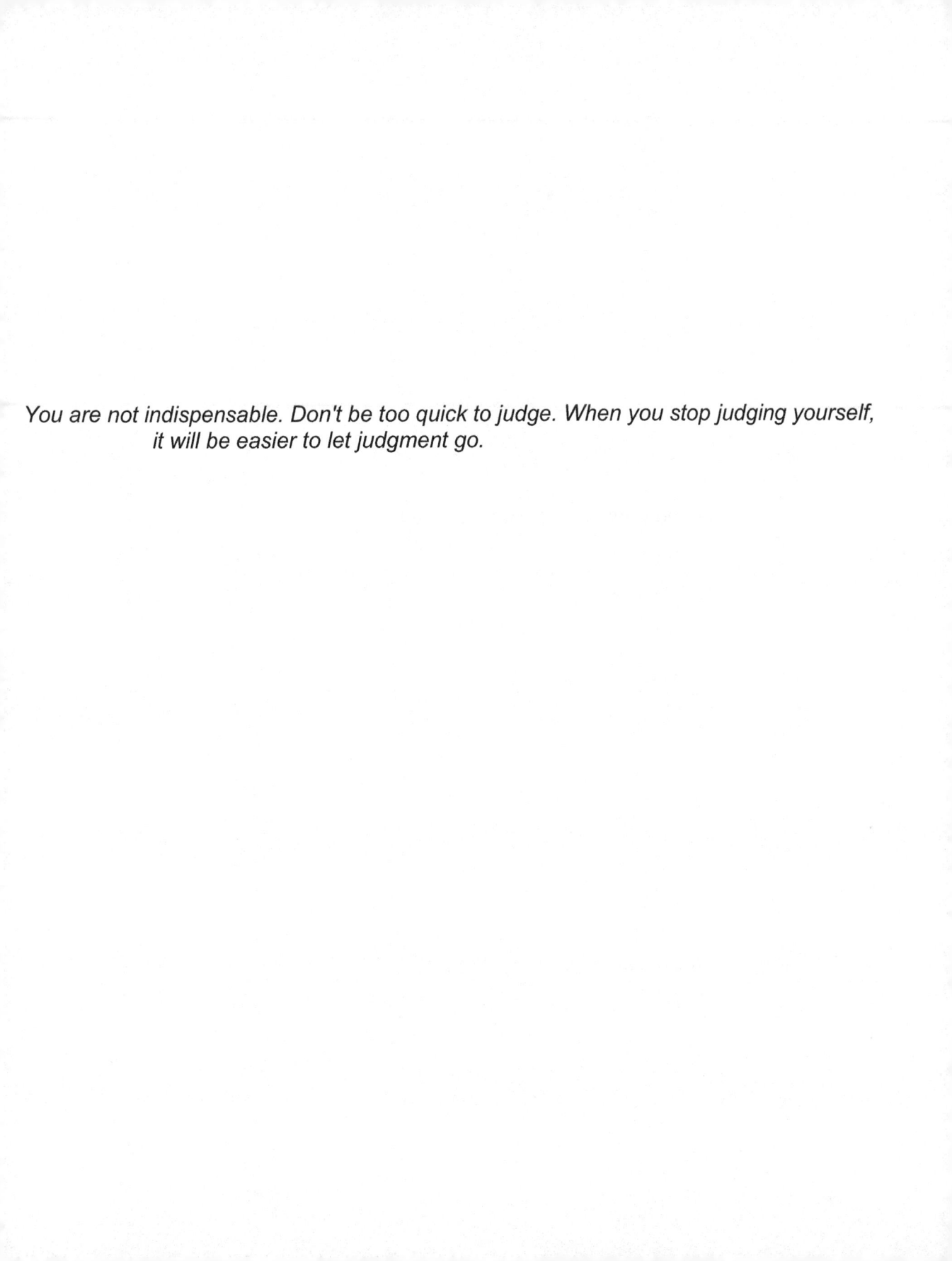

You are not indispensable. Don't be too quick to judge. When you stop judging yourself, it will be easier to let judgment go.

Stop making yourself feel like the villain.

Let God be the focus.

Chapter 2: You are the Mission.

God is always on standby; there's nothing to worry about. He's with you through it all.

It's essential to get to know God for yourself and your loved ones.

Worrying about people talking or lying to you will never attract anything good to you. Expand your mind to a different place where there is peace.

A negative thought will produce a negative, releasing a negative atmosphere. Purge it out of your heart daily, every second and minute. Try not to drop the ball. It's okay to start over again. If you forget, remember it all starts with a thought.

A move of God is on the way. The key to shaking back your life will be praying, that God's will be done in your life. There is nothing impossible to God. Allow Him to help you receive happiness and release all stress. Depend on nothing but the will of God and your faith.

Surround yourself with things that bring you happiness. Be present and visualize the moment. Even if your situation is not changing, don't fault yourself or anyone.

Keep applying yourself in every area. See yourself coming out. Speak positive thoughts.

Allow forgiveness in your heart.

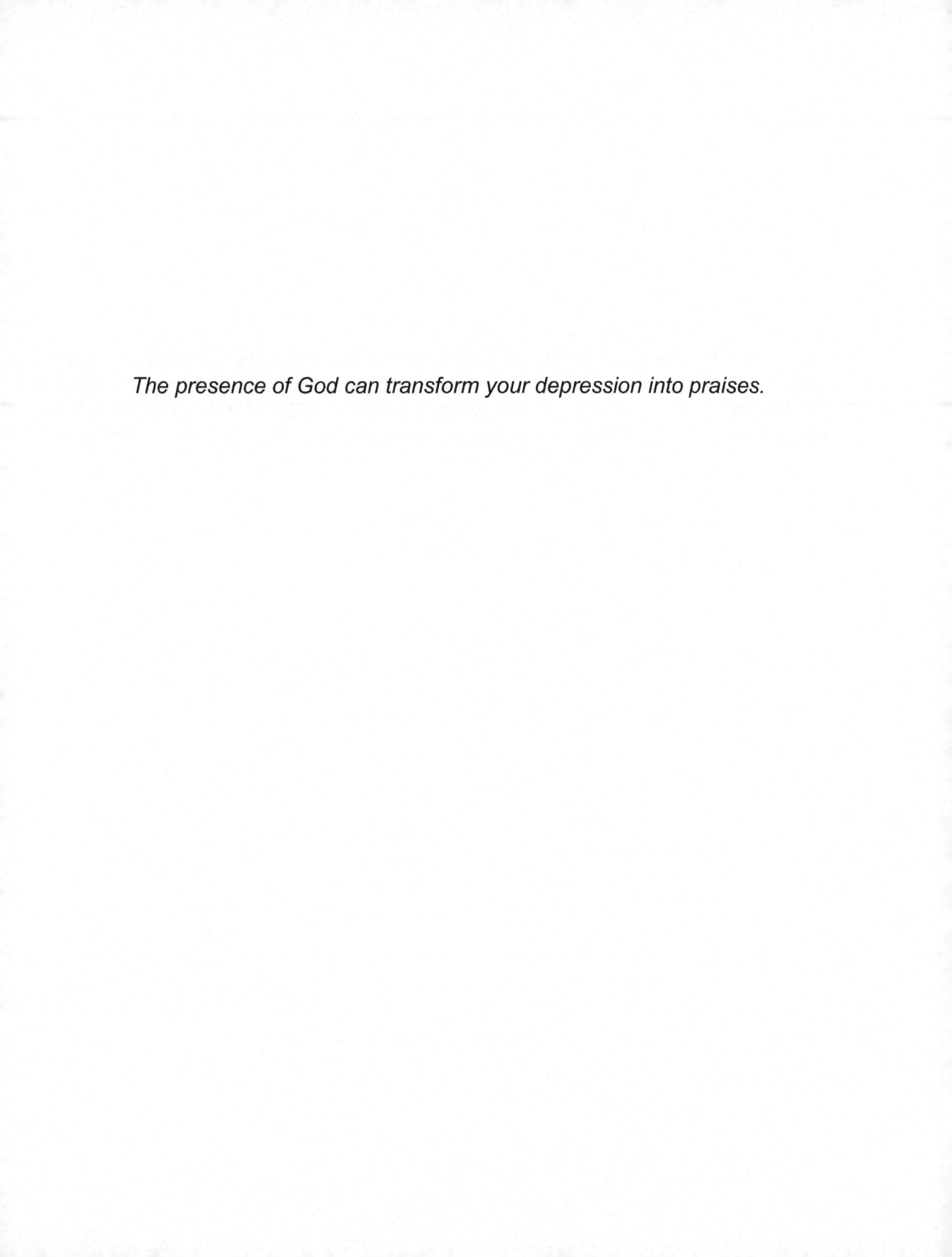

The presence of God can transform your depression into praises.

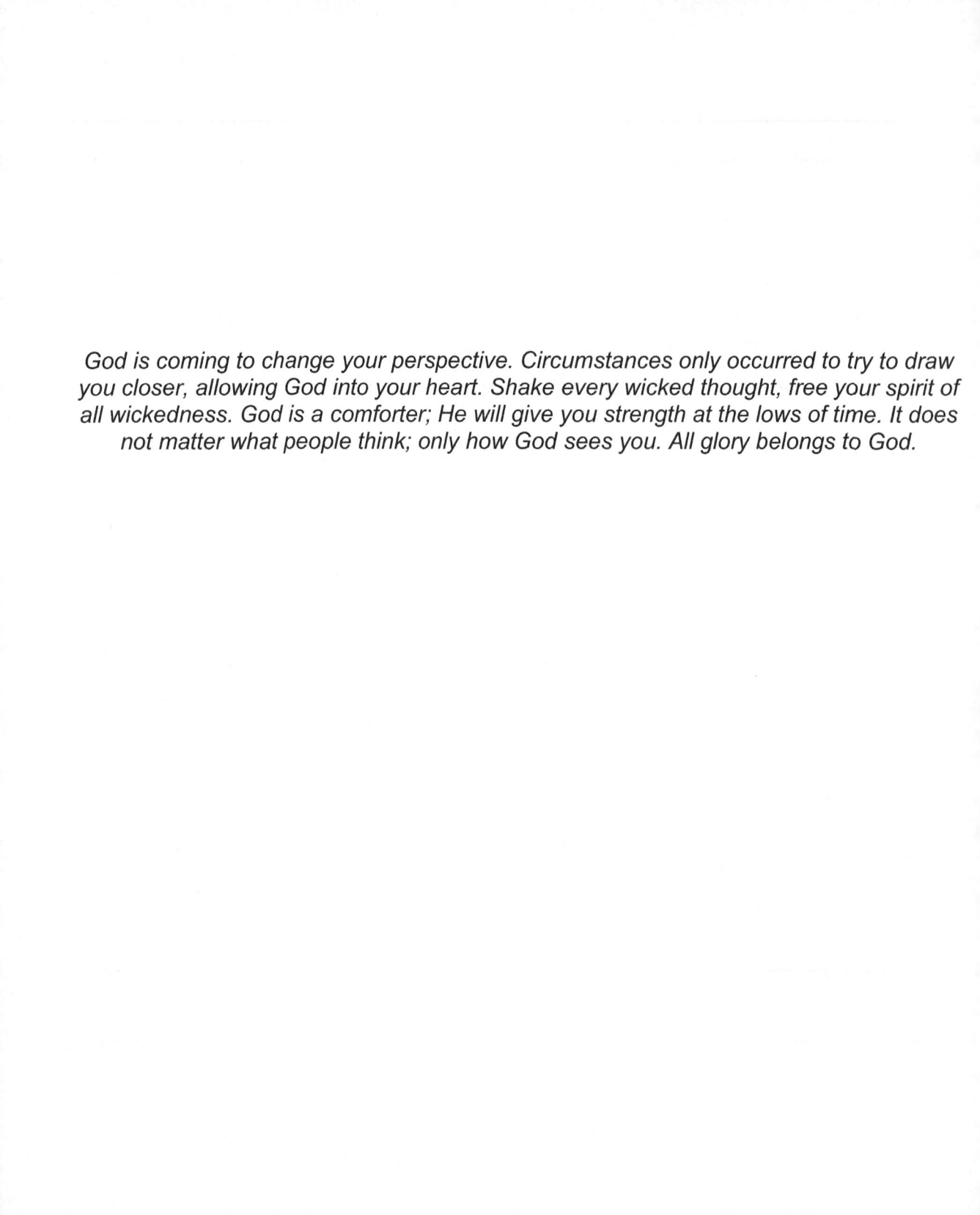

God is coming to change your perspective. Circumstances only occurred to try to draw you closer, allowing God into your heart. Shake every wicked thought, free your spirit of all wickedness. God is a comforter; He will give you strength at the lows of time. It does not matter what people think; only how God sees you. All glory belongs to God.

You are enclosed with so many terrific gifts. God handcrafted you with love, skills, the ability to stand, and with a beautiful heart. Your life adds value everywhere you go. In addition, you have access to the heavenly Father.

Have patience with yourself. People will always have their eyes on you; influence them through your actions and words.

Come on, King and Queen. God is everything. Empowering words. If you do not know by now, you are God's prized possessions.

This is not the time to feel lonely or isolated from anyone, including your friends and family members. Understand that change will always take place.

Find what makes you happy and fuels your desire to thrive. Focus on that in every moment of your life.

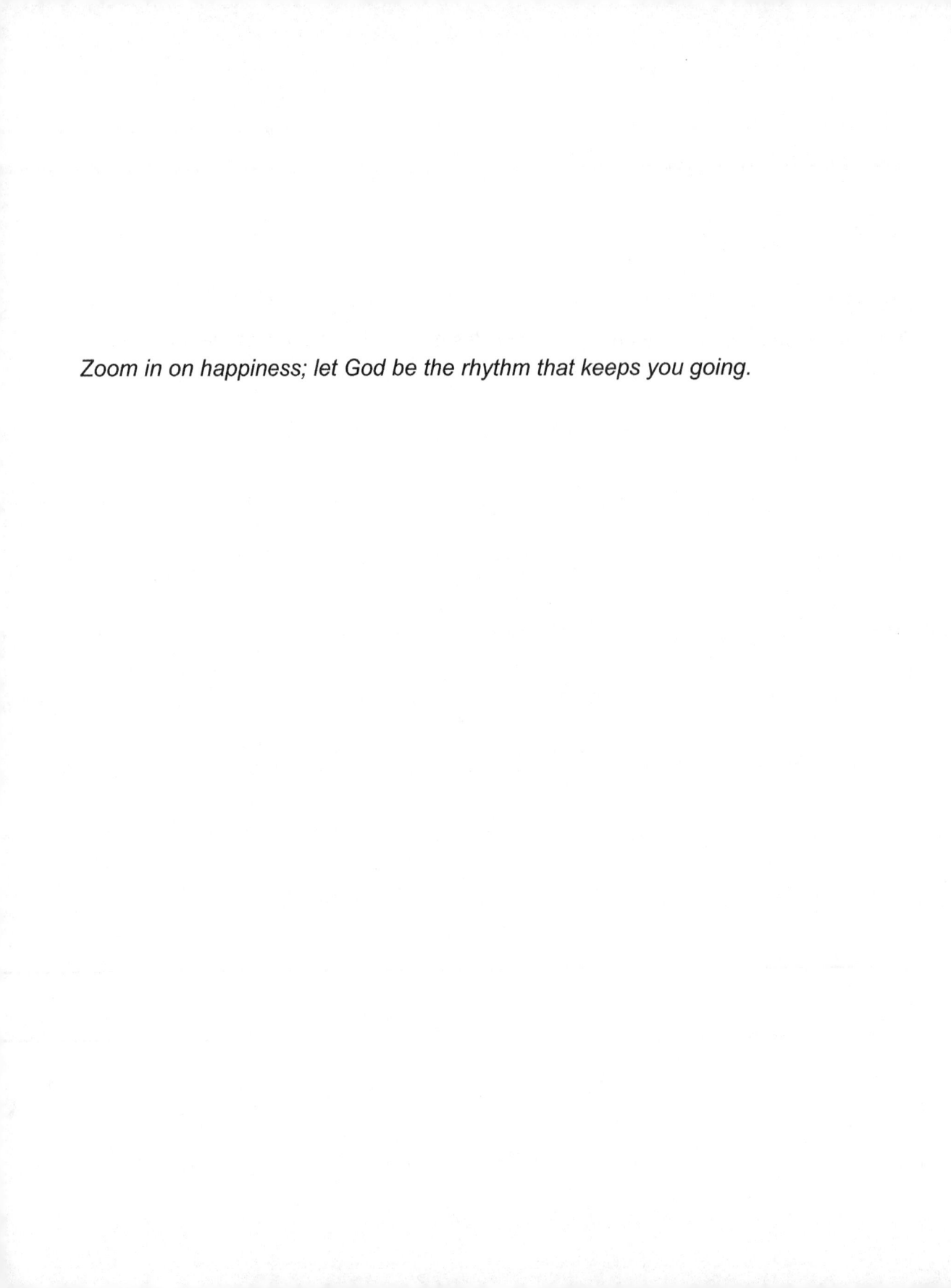

Zoom in on happiness; let God be the rhythm that keeps you going.

Keeping hope alive can be challenging at times; however, never stop focusing on your dreams.

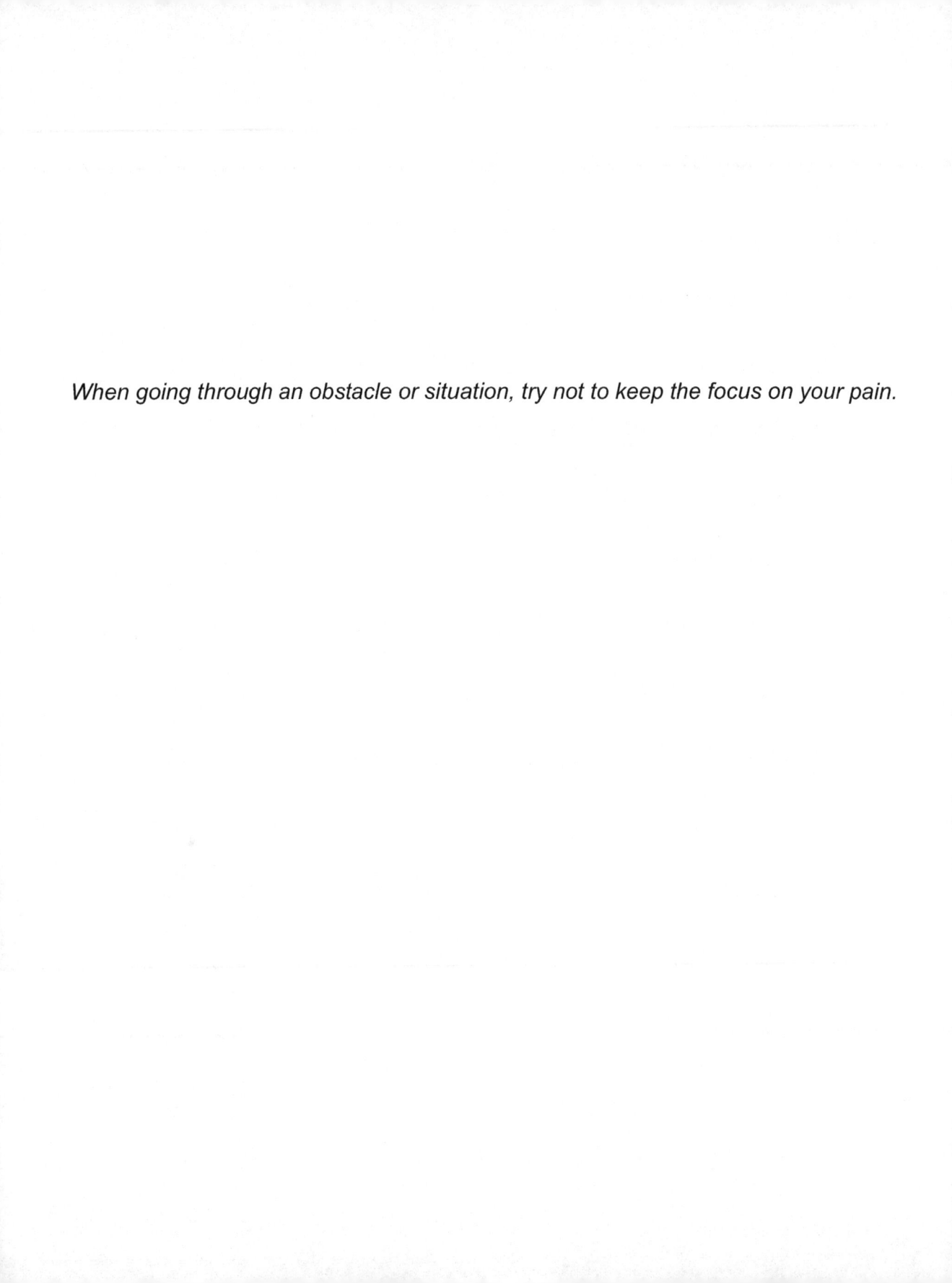

When going through an obstacle or situation, try not to keep the focus on your pain.

*Stop consuming negative thoughts about yourself. Just because a situation has taken place, there is no need to doubt yourself.
Invest more of your time with God and enhancing yourself. Do not focus on things that are dysfunctional and not good for your mental health.*

Surround yourself with encouraging experts whom you feel safe and secure with, such as family and friends. Be free."

Stay committed to avoiding stress.

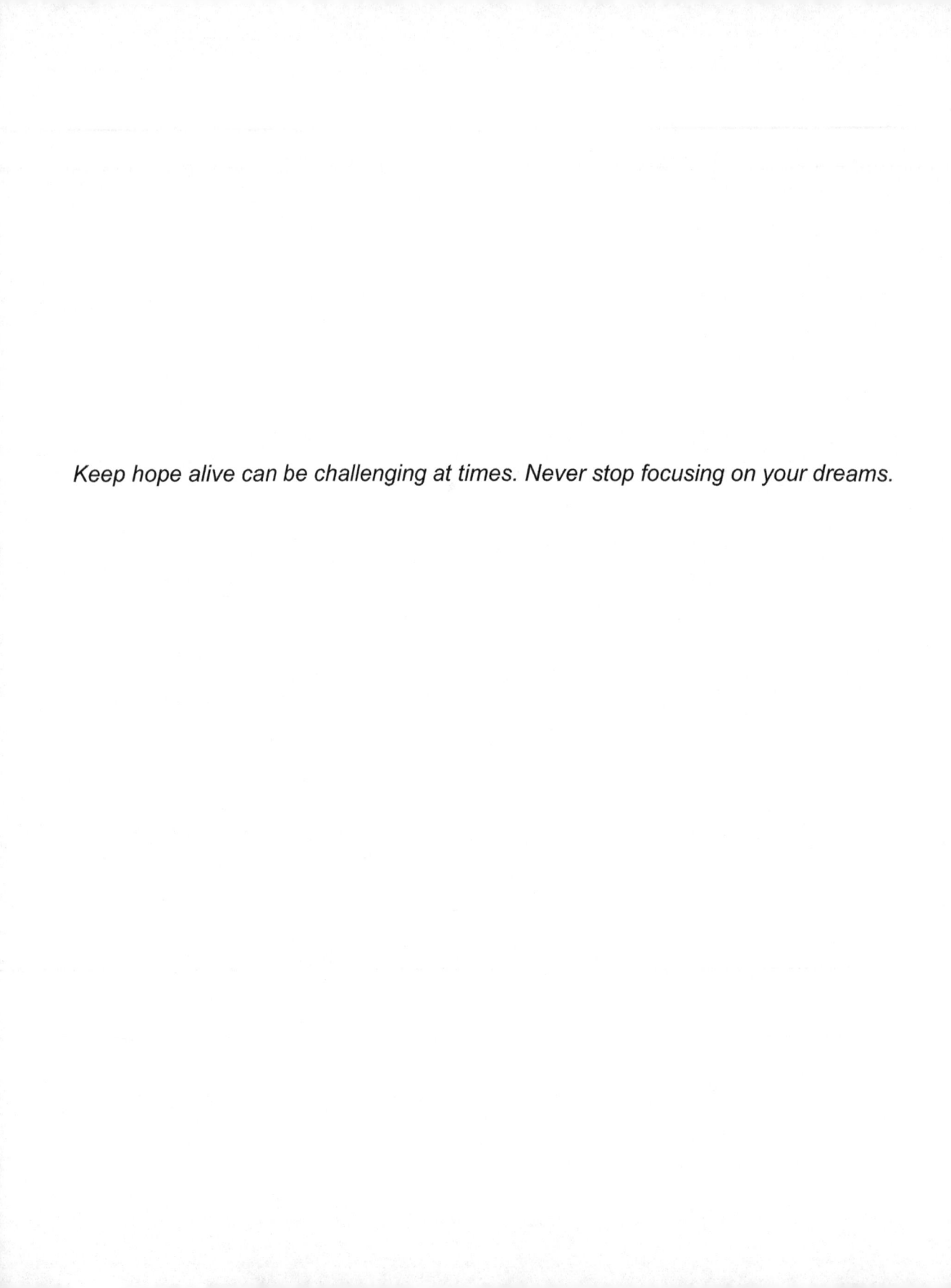

Keep hope alive can be challenging at times. Never stop focusing on your dreams.

Try letting go and giving it all to the Lord.

When horrible things come your way, avoid the chaos, then proceed with the mission in praise. Declare victory in troubled waters and ask the Lord to take His rightful place in your life.

Fill your temple with peace.

Shift your thought process and take action to fulfill your dreams and desires.

You will overcome difficulties; it won't magically happen—you'll have to put in the work. It's not just a dream.

Don't delay taking action; it's time to make a move.

Stop putting off and create.

Acknowledge bad experiences but focus on the good, especially with the people around you. If overwhelmed and stressed, let go of deep fears and vulnerabilities.

Don't let relationships, work, finances, friends, family members, etc., behavior cause you anxiety and worries.

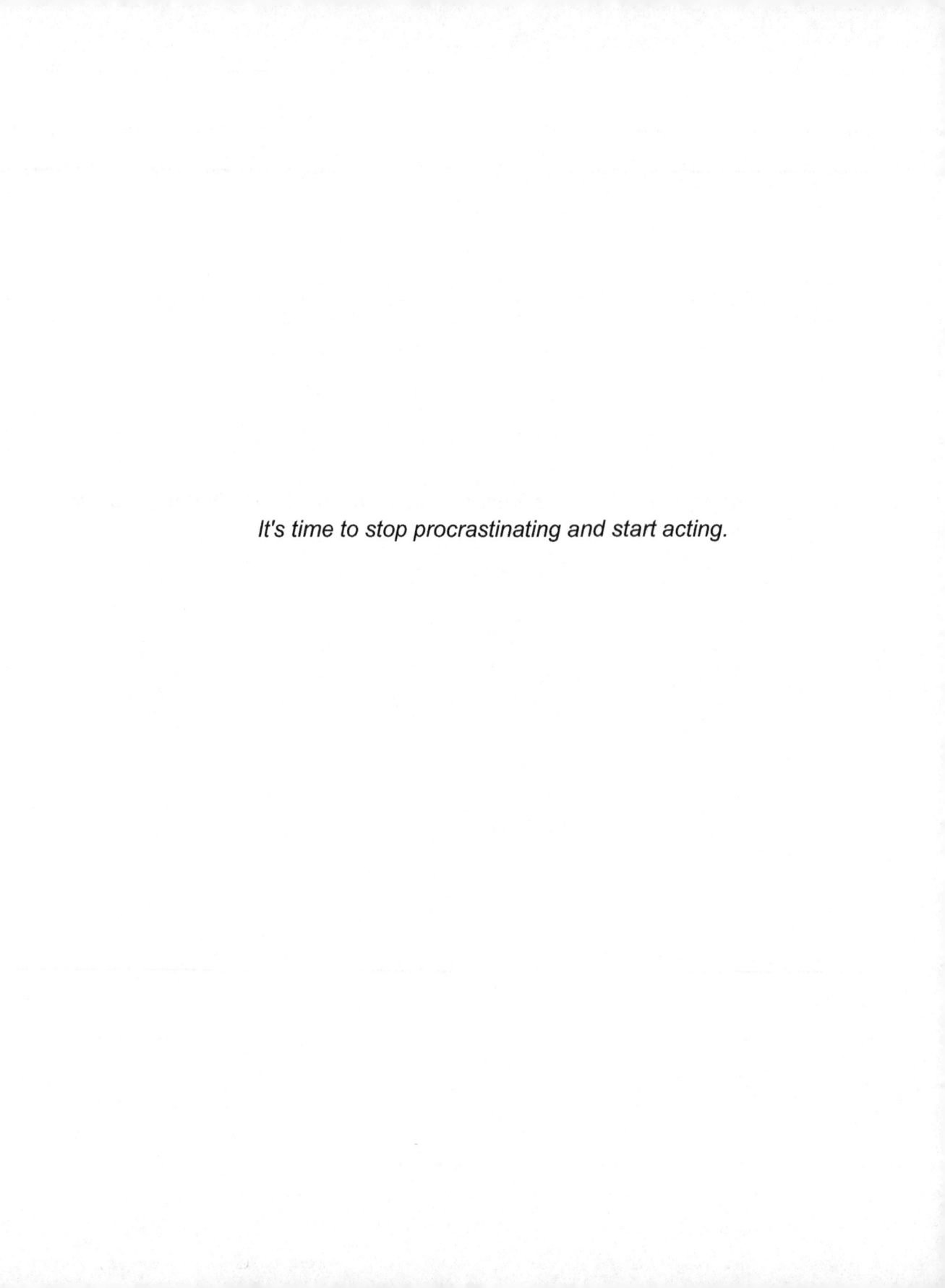

It's time to stop procrastinating and start acting.

Don't lose interest in yourself. Keep the torch going. There's a fire in you.

There's no need to rush things at this point. Try slowing down and doing things right. Let God in.

Exploring new territory is all about personal growth, which is critical because your soul requires guidance. Allow God's presence to show up.

Look for prosperity. Focus on the positive. Let good health, longevity, wisdom, and happiness overtake you every moment.

With God, He provides a word that adds hope and a peace that surpasses all understanding, nourishing your body with the fullness and satisfaction that only God can provide. On a positive note, seek God's presence.

It can be difficult to keep hope alive sometimes. Never stop focusing on your dreams. Stay focused on not stressing. It is important to get your healing so you can be the best version of yourself.

Just wanted to say, stay encouraged, and let nothing distract you from reaching your goals. Continue to be the best person I know you are, and always strive to love and blossom into the wonderful father, brother, son, mother, sister, or daughter that you can be. I'm proud of you. I know great things are happening in your life, and God knows the plans for you. You can overcome anything. You're not stuck or stagnant; you're right where you're supposed to be. Though you might not see it because your mind is on other things, you're building and shifting, more alert than ever. Have a great day!

God understands your needs and wants.

Take a break from yourself; block everything that doesn't feed your spirit in good health.

There are things in our minds we feel we lack. Listen to me, your mind is lacking nothing. Thank you, Lord.

I know you have a lack of trust.

It's good to take time and deal with the emotions that are inside of you.

Don't sleep on your dreams.

Let God's action move on your heart so that your reaction is worth it.

Take a stand; you are now walking side-by-side with God, denying negativity, pushing through, and letting go. Let nothing or no one control your mind and thoughts, not even trauma from your past. Stagnancy is not a part of your process anymore. Have a lot of fun in the process! It's all about having awareness; it is time to achieve personal growth.

What represents your sense of creativity? Apply your attention to your talents, your gifts, things that make you happy reading a book, taking a long walk, meditating on God's word. The thing that brings you happiness and enjoyment can always change but keep searching for it and applying it to your everyday life.

Whatever that thing is that brings joy, make more time to redirect your energy in a positive light, giving others the light of attraction that you want to receive. Make time to focus on others by spreading your light. God is the word in the time of darkness; therefore, reach out and touch someone else in the time of your storm and dark clouds. Be the light to stand out brighter than the star.

You never know what you have until it is gone; then the value of what you had changes.

You are loved. You are special to me, and I hold you very dearly in my heart. I wish and pray for nothing but the best for you and your family. God holds you in a place higher than you can think and imagine. I am so grateful to have you, and God loves you dearly. The Lord allowed me and other people the ability to see your beautiful soul full of special gifts and blessings.

Testimony

"We, as people, will experience temporary hurt and pain. Joy and sorrow will come, but God, I just love you and your sweet spirit and soul. I don't know if I ever told you about the time of my life when I experienced stage three cancer. I thought my life was over, and I was literally on my deathbed in my head. Despite that, I spoke life over myself. I know that God had a plan bigger than this life. Currently, everything inside of me has died, but God. I am here just to say that God restored me, and He would do the same for you."

God holds the key to everything you need; He will guide you, and your subconscious mind holds the master key, providing you with the roadmap. However, it's ultimately about free will.

Teach me how to work on not stressing.

It's difficult to keep hope alive sometimes. Never stop focusing on your dreams. Don't focus on stressing; please try your best to let it go. God will continue to give us the strength that we need. Therefore, healing involves new ideas and clarity, as well as expanding our mind. Self-love never fails, so keep evolving. I am proud of you.

It's okay to just be you. You have the power to shift the atmosphere. You were born for greatness. Radiate nothing but good energy back to yourself and others, without self-reflecting upon others. No more invading other spaces with all your pain and trauma. Embrace them with your light. Have control of your thoughts by invading your negative thoughts with something beautiful, placing them in a space filled with love and light.

It's your time to shine constantly. Let the love and light surround you.

Less worrying about people talking and lying on you. Negative thoughts will never attach to anything good. Expand your mind to a different place where there is peace. Let self-love grow and emerge into something beautiful.

Chapter 3: Peace of mind

God will restore anybody. God gives us joy and peace. I feel that life is not fair. It is not, but God's plan and his justice for this earth have already won the battle. There are no words that I can say, but God, my heart is heavy at times, but my faith is strong. I know your faith is high. God is the only one that I know we can call on at any given moment. When things get hot and bothered, when things shake me up, I had to find my place and rest in Him. I had to vent about it and release it because the issue no longer is mine. God can help us.

We allow our issues and other people's issues to become a problem. Then, as humans, we take it into our own hands and make it our issues. Eventually, it becomes our focus and turns into our problems.

God loves you, no matter what.

Indeed, God cares.

Allow God to be the heart of your soul.

Embrace personal peace.
Rest in peace.
Allow peace to be your personal journey.

Furthermore, I know you are breaking chains. Besides, I know you are a conqueror. Life is a journey full of hope, love, beauty, scars, and self-discovery. I have touched the freedom bell in some areas of my life. You have also rung the freedom bell in your life. But most times, we are stuck in our own heads. Every day is a new chapter, and God's spirit is here to help us all. God will bless you with a blessing out of it all, even through the painful and suffering. Down the line, God always had a plan; He never left us. God allows us to connect, and I am grateful for your life. I am here to embrace you with love and encouragement.

*Great ideas come from the Lord.
Only you know what you like and needed.*

Know your self-worth. Be proud of all you've accomplished.

Know that you are capable of overcoming anything; giving up on yourself is not an option.

Have faith that everything is going to work out for your highest good.

Whatever happens in your life, choose to find happiness in every situation.

Always focus on creating happy feelings.

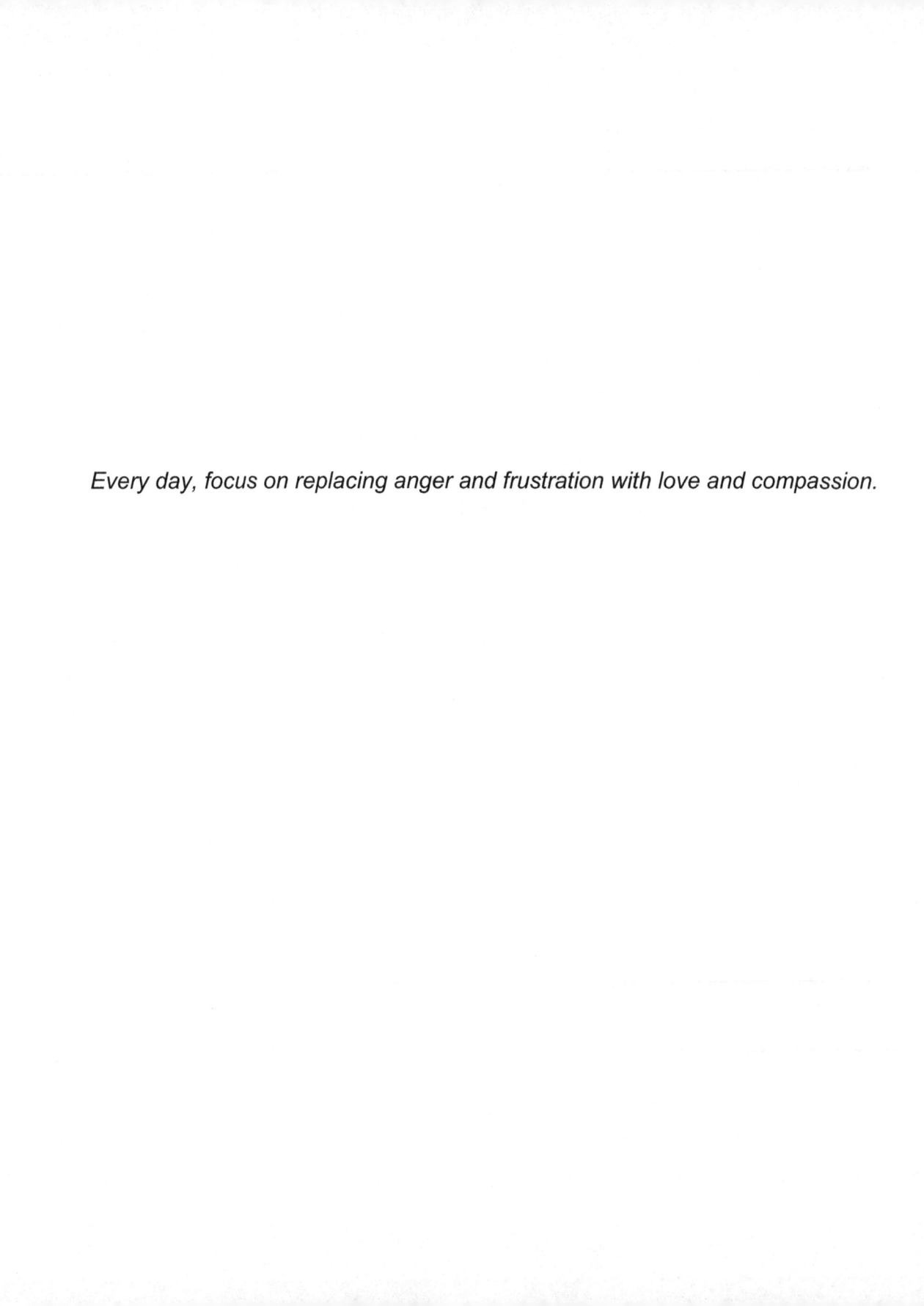

Every day, focus on replacing anger and frustration with love and compassion.

Learn to trust that your intuition will lead you in the right direction. Be willing to open yourself up to trust the journey. No matter your choices or circumstances, choose to stay calm. Always be excited about every fresh start.

The Most High will always bring you comfort wherever you go. Keep being determined to become the best version of yourself you can be. Always live in the present. Keep filling your days with activities that bring you joy.

There is the life that you live, and then there is the life that you want. Continue to take action to align with your dreams. If you want something, never stop dreaming. Occasionally, you have to do different things to obtain a different result.

Know that you are worthy of financial stability. In no time at all, you will be far down the road. Be excited about what is coming next in your life. You have always gotten through every bad day of life, and you are undefeated.

Be determined and intentional. God is everlasting. Just think positive and always affirm how good and amazing God is. You are living proof of what the mercy of God can do. We are all still here to tell the story. We all have overcome something, only because of His goodness and mercy.

There will always be things that we all have to endure, but we have to stay focused because God has a plan.

Love yourself in the midst of your storm.

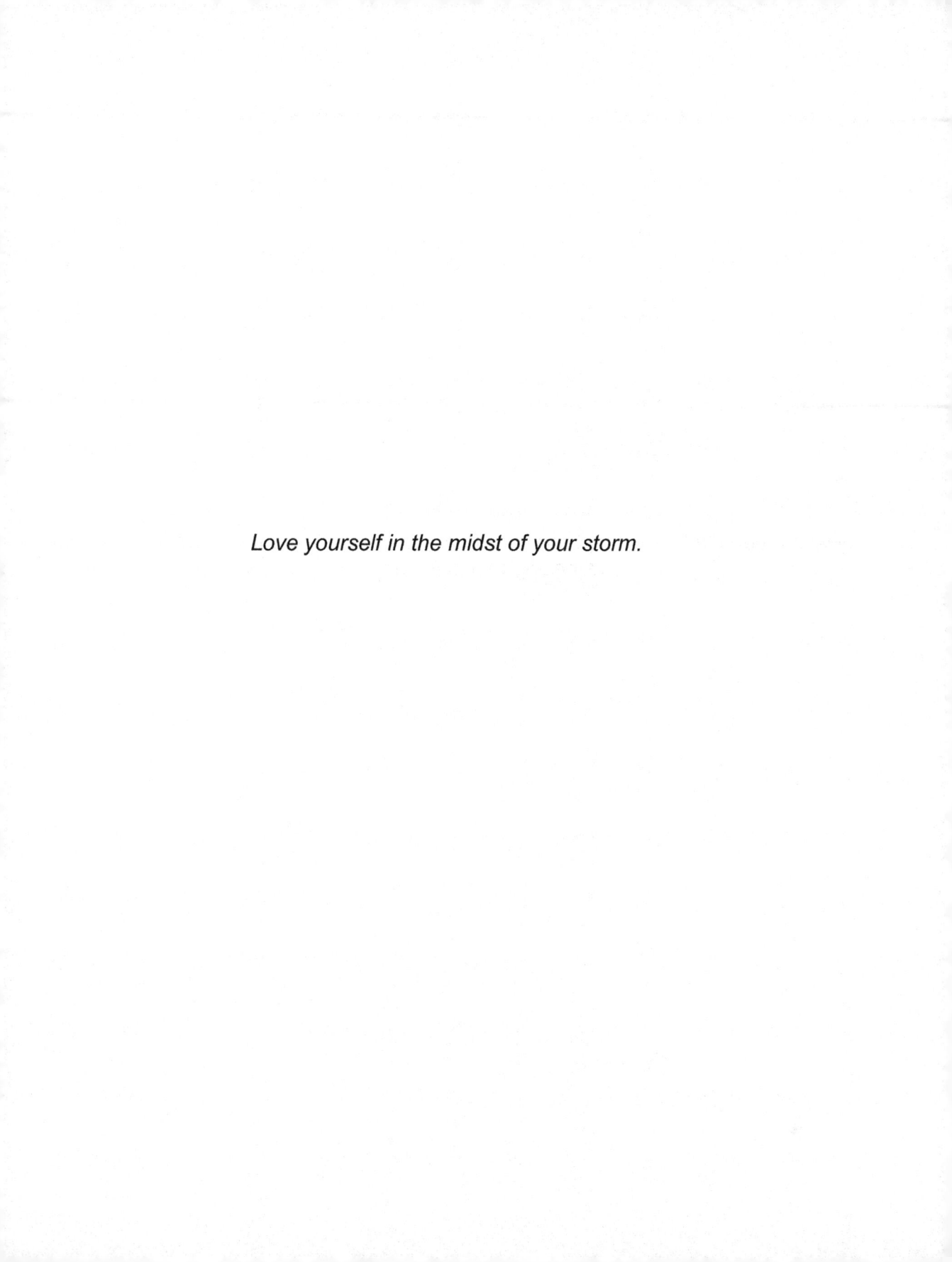

Have a beautiful day! Keep your head up and remember to think positive; God has amazing things in store for you.

What are you birthing during your pain?

If you feel God is talking to you, do not hesitate when He is in your presence.

I don't know what you see when you look in the mirror, but what I do know is that you are beautiful inside and out

Life-changing experiences can happen every day; embrace them along with the change.

Lord, help me. What would you like me to do with this life?

God is the world's biggest torch. He is a pathway full of light, joy, and happiness, offering healing for our souls and peace to our thoughts.

Take time to grow, and your light will shine.

God first. He has you in a special place in his heart and know that you're in my heart as well. Your intuition is very magical and powerful. God is growing you spiritually and upwards. Keep moving in the direction that is giving you peace because God said he is going to restore happiness and prosperity.

Keep moving in the direction that is giving you peace because God is going to restore your happiness and prosperity.

Our trials are meant to make us better human beings, so that we can depend on God for ourselves and not humankind. Because of God's mercy, we can recognize the opportunities of letting God's will be done. Lord, my praises are for real.

I am so proud of you.

Your life will tell a beautiful story.

Let it happen, feel your heart, and have a wonderful day. Sometimes life is a struggle, but with God! Every day presents a different obstacle. Keep letting your light shine! Let nothing cloud your thoughts. I pray that peace continues to surround you and good health.

If you feel God is talking to you, do not hesitate when He is in your presence.

Our Father in Heaven is always watching over us; have no worries.

For some people, praying comes naturally; for others, it has to be something major to happen to shift them to pray. We all have the gift, and sometimes it does not light up until God activates it.

There are so many terrific gifts in you. God handcrafted you with love, skills, the ability to stand, and a beautiful heart. Your life adds value everywhere you go. In addition, you have access to heaven on earth.

Be strong and courageous, because in time it will all work out. At some point, we all face adversity, discouragement, and disappointment throughout life. We must endure life's challenges. We are not alone; God is just drawing us closer to Him. God is right there with us, standing to protect us.

Do not let your mind take you to a messed-up place. You deserve peace. Do not allow your mind to stop you from seeing the mercy and miracles of God. This is not the season to compare. Do not rob yourself of your own joy. I am convinced that God can pull us out of anything, especially our thought process. No more sabotaging.

In life, we have to help others to help ourselves. It's all a part of God's plan. God possesses supreme authority. The Lord is going to see you through. We have to build others up in the process of looking for ourselves. The reflection is beautiful. When we can help others, we can also find ourselves. Believe and know you are worthy and unique. Try not to stay in your feelings and emotions. You have to find out what makes you special and happy. God places people in your life to help, as well as vice versa for them to help you. You are part of a beautiful journey. When you are not sure, just trust that you are making a difference in people's lives. It is all part of the process. Everything is working out.

Chapter 4: Healing from Within

Always focus on what is right. Let the cessation of happiness lead you on the right path to God. Keep scribing to doing what is right. You are responsible for your soul. If you get off the course, God is the key to finding your way back.

*It is hard to keep hope alive sometimes.
Never stop focusing on your dreams.*

Be determined and intentional. God is everlasting. Just think positive and always affirm how good and amazing God is. You are living proof of what the mercy of God can do.

Like all the other great names throughout history, you have what it takes to reach your highest potential. I believe in you as well as myself. No time to stop. God is in the blessing business. No matter the season you are in, there is always a problem with the information the Devil provides. Remember that the Devil will always be an underhanded snake. Please go to God. You can always go back to God and try again. He will always provide you with awesome information. When you need Him, you can count on Him at any time.

Thank God, I am no longer pointing the finger at God. I am no longer pointing the finger at myself. No more hurting me.

Think of nothing but good moments every time you feel like your mind is slipping away. Recall all the good moments throughout your day. It always helps to keep a smile on your face. When you are a child of God, you are never alone in your thoughts. A child of God always has to think twice, once for themselves and once to make sure they heard God's voice. Despite the things we have to endure, we have to stay strong.

Oh yes, I can. Oh yes, oh yes, He will. I will proceed daily to build my strength, strengthen my faith, rely on the Father. I will first consider my feelings, advise my thinking, dedicate time to encourage, motivate, and, instead of hate, create love and peace all around me physically, mentally, and emotionally.

You are amazing. I just love the heart and spirit that you have. Keep thriving for excellence. Pour out goodness because blessings are all around you; there is always someone watching. You are a good man, baby; you are a good man. Time is important with one another. Love you, thank you again.

Who knows you better than you know yourself? Do not let people manipulate you into believing that you don't know who you are. You are a living testimony designed by God's perfect grace. There's nothing wrong with you—seek clarity. The answers are within you; ask God to activate them as you journey through life. Challenges aren't meant to hurt you but to help you identify who you truly are. Stay true to yourself, be all that you can be. Will you be who you are, or will you be who others want you to be?

Sometimes life makes you get dirty so that we can value God eventually, as well as learn to value people. The perspective is different, the purpose is different. God wants to use the situations for our good, in hopeful that we will follow God.

Don't forget your worth, a beautiful heart comes with a process. Life has a process season, and God shows up just for your reminder. Always self-reflect and forgive yourself and others, just how God made you.

God makes us uncomfortable so that we can be a blessing to someone else. Self-care makes everything better.

God is everything and everywhere and is on time.

Bad things happen. Do you trust God in the midst of everything that He allowed to happen? God is moving. God wants to move your heart and spirit. God is preparing you for greatness. Get ready. There is nothing but miracles coming your way.

God loves you not only for what you are but for everything that makes you. You are perfect in God's eyes!

Continue to move forward, regardless of what comes your way. Do not get discouraged. God is in the midst of everything, and His plan is to draw us closer and closer to Him.

Blessings are falling. Continue to smile no matter what.

It is our choices and responsibility to confirm and know what God means to us.

Trust the process and the possibility.

God knows what He is doing, and I trust His plan. You are perfect. You are wonderful, made in the image of God, no matter how your mind tells you that you are not.

You are amazing. I just love the heart and spirit that you have. Keep thriving for excellence. Pour out goodness because blessings are all around you; there is always someone watching.

Time is important with one another. Keep loving.

God showing up just for your reminder. Always self-reflect and forgive yourself and others, just as God will.

God makes us uncomfortable so that we can be a blessing to someone else. Self-care makes everything better. God is everything and everywhere and is on time.

Do not lose your faith.

Bad things happen. Do you trust God amid everything that He allowed to happen?

God is moving.

God wants to move your heart and spirit.

God is preparing you for greatness. Get ready.

There is nothing but miracles coming your way.

So, therefore, the agonizing or vexed feeling is attached to what aggravates your spirit, people around.

God loves you not only for what you are but for everything that makes you. You are perfect in God's eyes!

It is our choices and responsibility to confirm and know what God means to us.

Trust the process and the possibility.

God is going to turn it around. Lord, forgive me and help me forgive myself.

Remember that God has ordained every footstep you've taken, even if you thought it was a detour. God was pushing you into your blessing.

Like the old people say, "Peace, be still, Father." I know who I am, and I have come to a place where all I can do is pour out thank you, God. All we are to do is hear and seek a word from God. Do you know the key to praise your way out? Sing, dance, laugh, get your freedom back. You are worthy to be happy, and He is worthy to be praised. It goes hand-in-hand with praise and worship, the option to a successful path. When you are ready to release and let all the sorrows and burdens go, you will feel the release. The only order: you are a walking miracle. There is no stronghold in your mind. You are healed; the world is playing a new illusion.

There is no one that can get your mind out of the space that you are in but you and God. However, feel a breakthrough coming your way. It is a mighty move of God. Please let it change your day. Whatever your spirit is asking for, only you can fulfill it. God is always waiting on us.

One thing I can say:

Lord, forgive me and help me forgive myself.

What should be a necessity is your happiness. Lord, forgive me and help me forgive myself.

No matter how hard the journey gets, do not let the headaches, pain, and seemingly overwhelming obstacles produce depressing moments. It is all just temporary; it is trying to paralyze your mind. You have to keep moving. Your journey is bigger than what you can see. You have accomplished so much, and there is still so much to come. It is just the beginning. I am just so happy to be a part.

I am so proud to know you. I am happy to have you as a friend. Furthermore, I am so happy about the relationship; you have shown me that dreams come true even in silence. God continues to move even when it does not look like everything is perfect on the outside. However, God is shaping it all together for your good. I want you to know that you are an extraordinary person, and God created you for greatness. He is constantly and will continue to show up in your life. There is nothing you can do to stop Him from showing up. So keep being you, keep loving those who come around you, and know that God is in the midst of everything that He does. Amen.

As within, good thoughts; as without, good thoughts.

All that we have to do is hear the word of God, praise, and worship. Let all the sorrows and burdens go to find peace. You are the key from within to without. Hear and seek God's word, praise, and worship Him. Then release, let all the sorrows and burdens go. That is the only order; no one can heal you but you. No one can get your mind out of the space that it is in but you. Be aware of who comes around you and know that God is in the midst of everything that He does. Amen.

Don't get caught up in your current circumstances.

You are an overcomer.

Chapter 5: Trust Yourself

I need more of your will. You're amazing. Keep moving one step at a time. Be mindful of everyone who comes around you and know that God is in the midst of everything that He does. Amen.

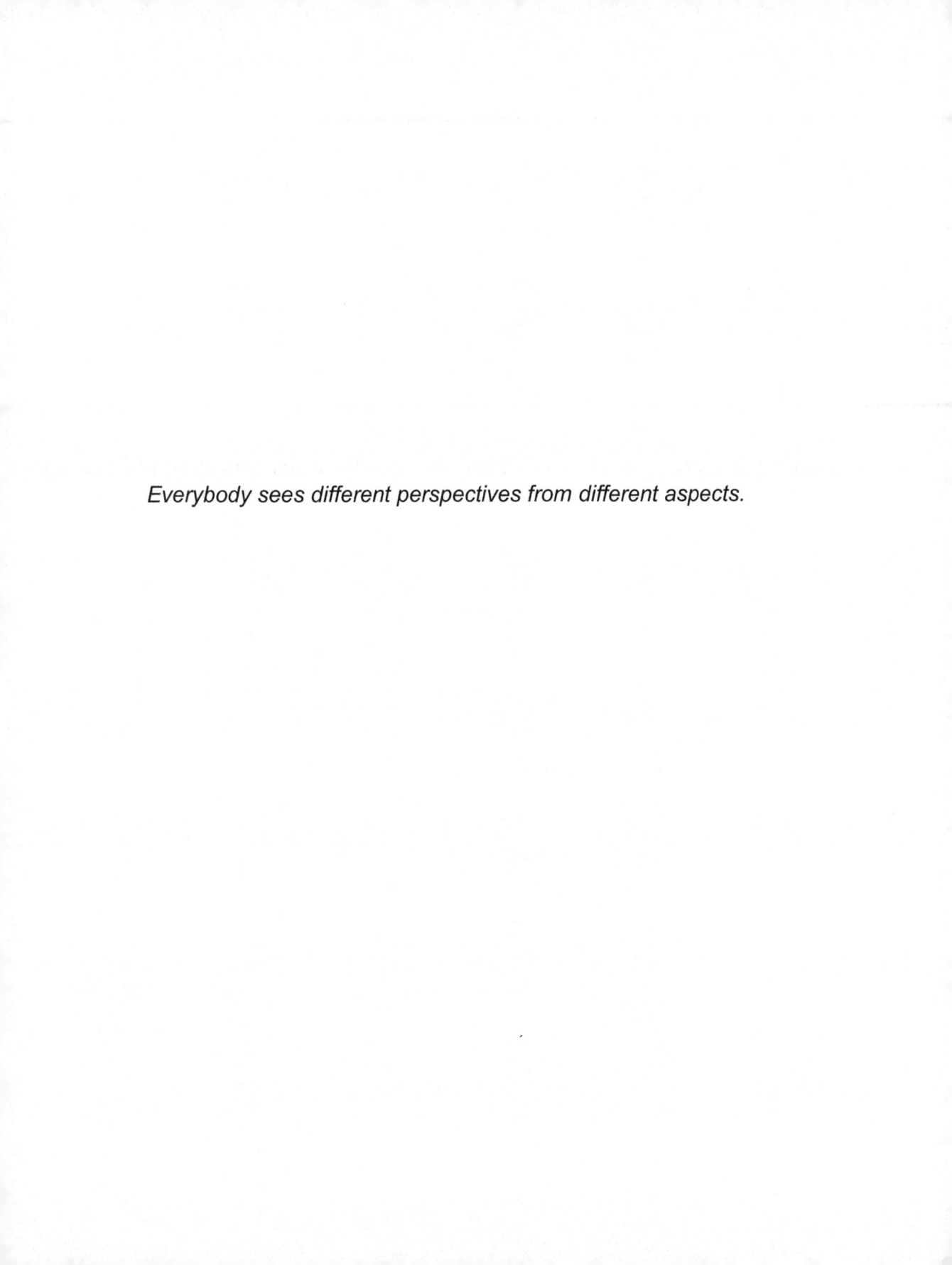

Everybody sees different perspectives from different aspects.

You never know what you have until it is gone, then the value of what you had changes.

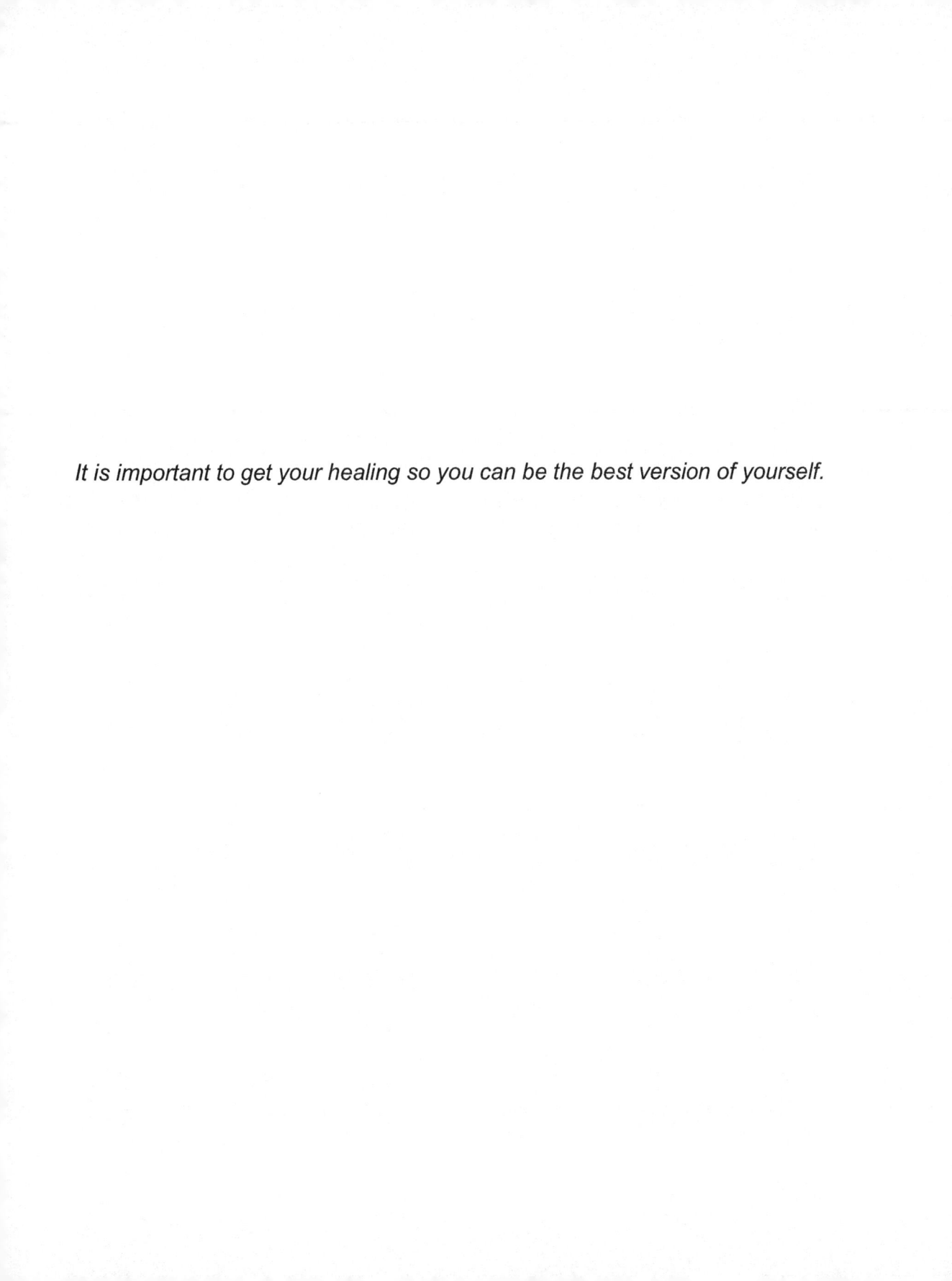

It is important to get your healing so you can be the best version of yourself.

It is difficult to keep hope alive sometimes. Never stop focusing on your dreams. Don't focus on stressing; please try your best to let it go.

God will continue to give us the strength that we need; therefore, healing involves new ideas and clarity, as well as expanding our minds.

Self-love never fails, so keep evolving. I am proud of you.

God is very vital to our life.

Stressing has no purpose.

I have one question for you: Do you love yourself more?

You are already equipped, born for greatness.

Find something else to do with your frustration; make something beautiful out of your pain. You will only get this time once in a lifetime.

I rebuke the enemy in his tracks right now; nothing is going to stop you. God has mercy and grace upon your life. He has already revealed to you what you need to do to accomplish a new mission. That time and date have expired. Rest in peace.

God is not waiting on your approval.

The revelations to your blessings are within you. God is your strength. Life requires patience. You will have to learn to shed the parts of your life that are not relevant, release the pain, and let forgiveness in.

God is making way for your new path and a fresh start.

If you cannot release, you cannot receive. But there's more to it than that; you will have to let other things go. If you desire wealth and peace, add forgiveness to your heart.

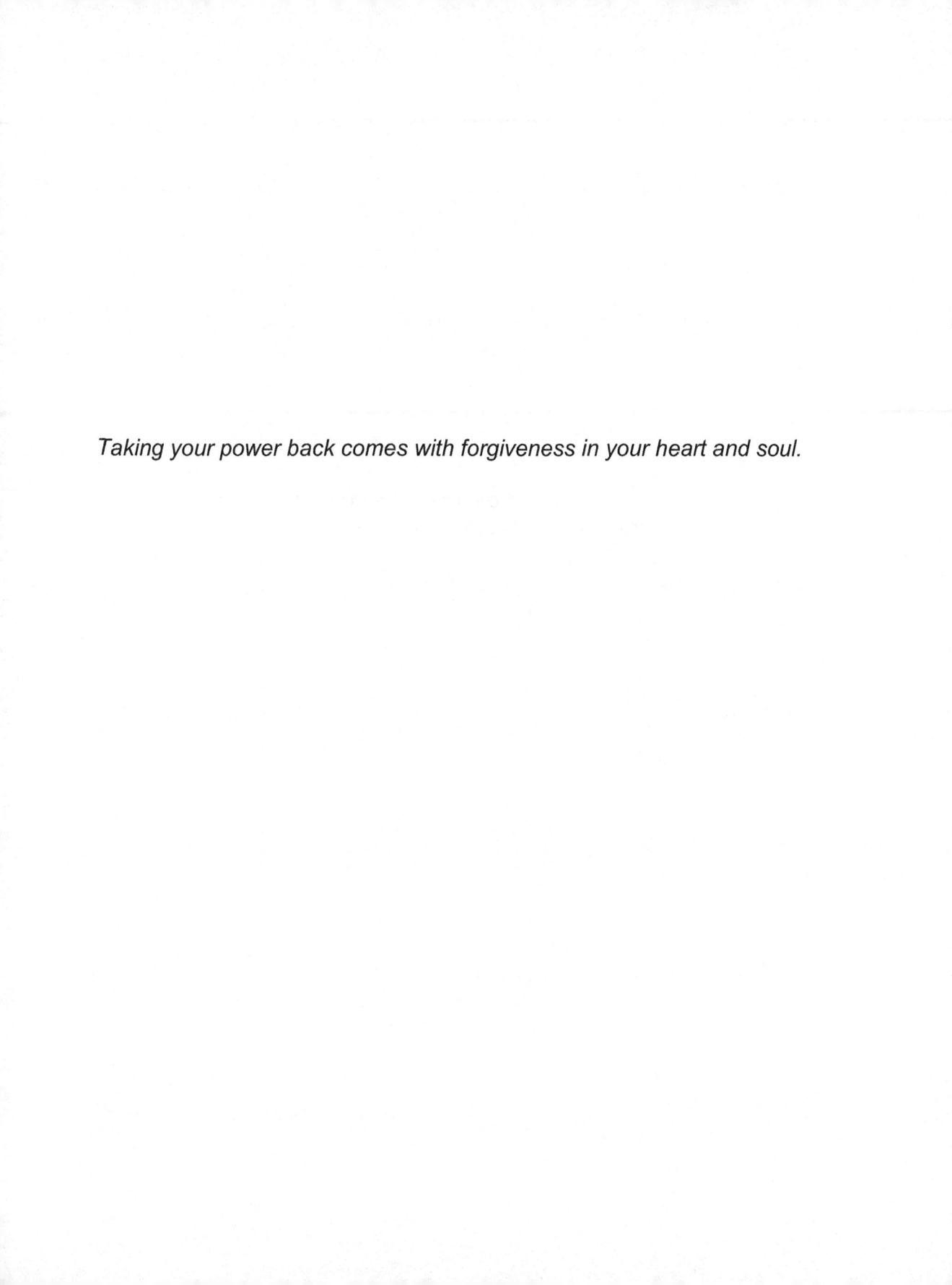

Taking your power back comes with forgiveness in your heart and soul.

*Continue to embrace the right love.
Keep trusting in yourself.*

You are the key.

Stop suppressing the past thoughts.

Maybe you are noticing other people's energy. All is well with you.

God is the key to everything. Jesus is the blueprint to life.

Your life has value all by itself.

Unapologetically be yourself.

Pray in every season because you are coming out.

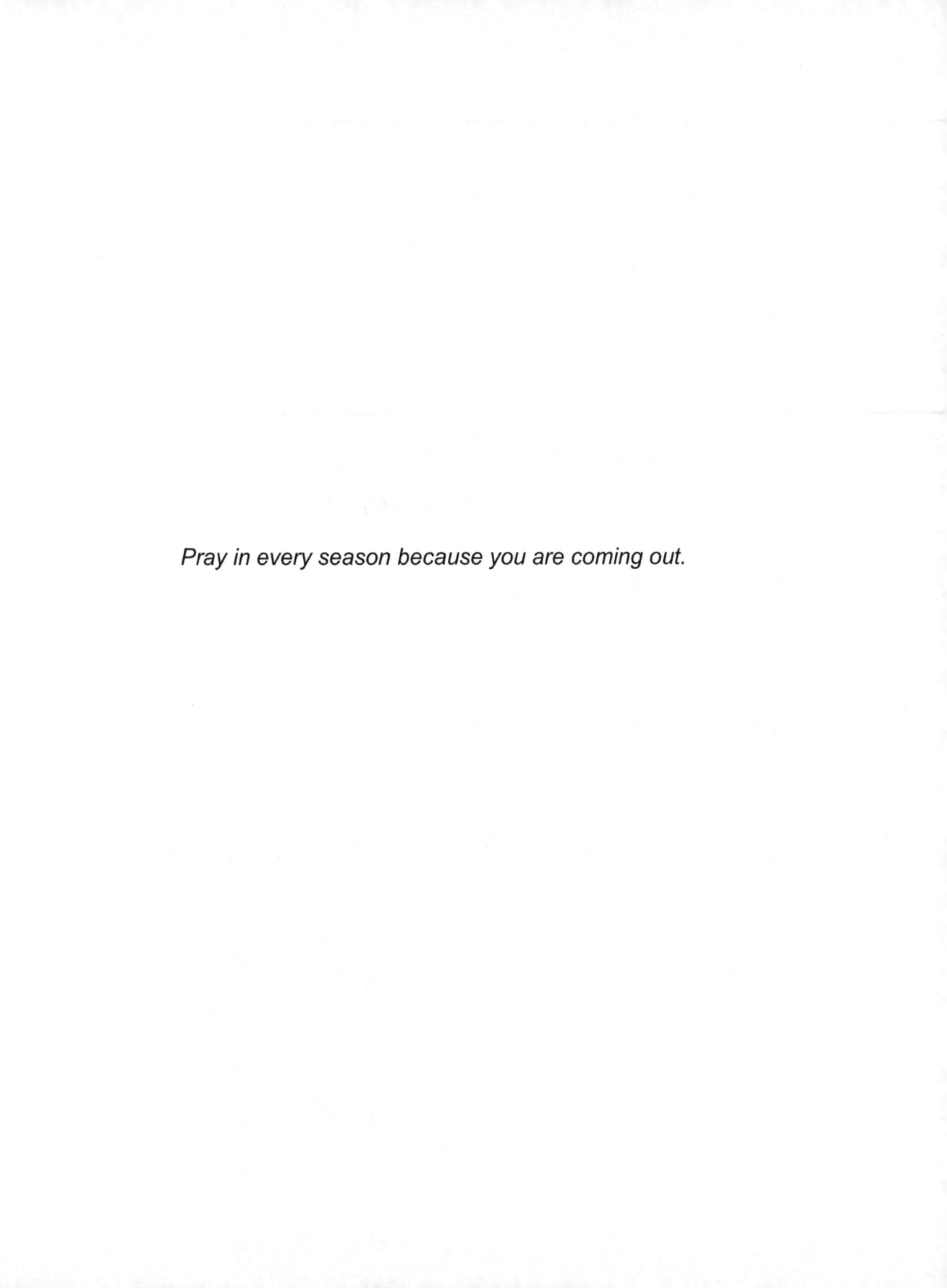

Unapologetically be yourself.

It's ok to laugh.

I wonder what would happen if I started taking God seriously.

Don't have time for mess; I'm trying to find freedom in my mind.

Planning is not easy, but it is necessary.

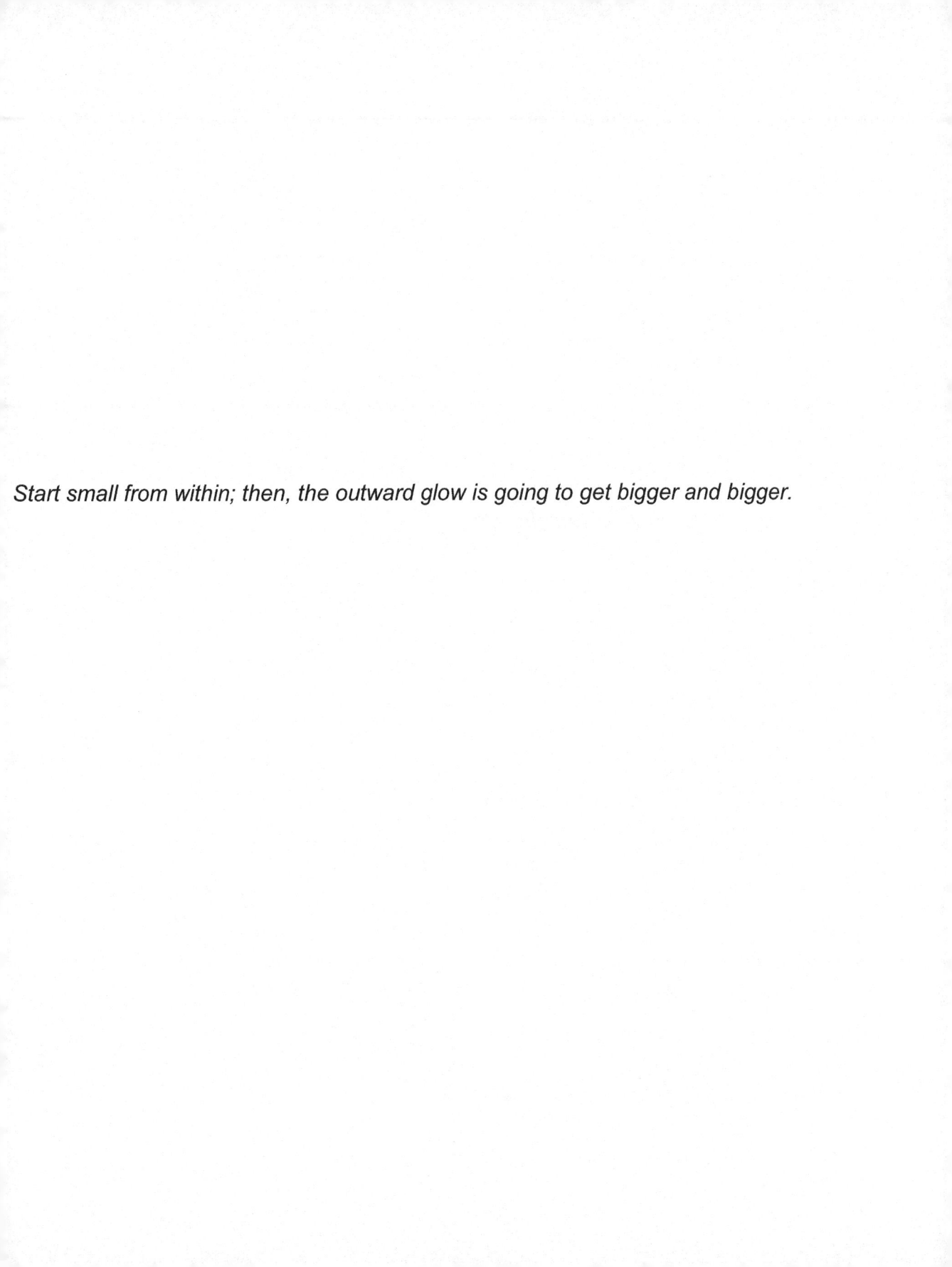

Start small from within; then, the outward glow is going to get bigger and bigger.

Keep your thoughts clear.

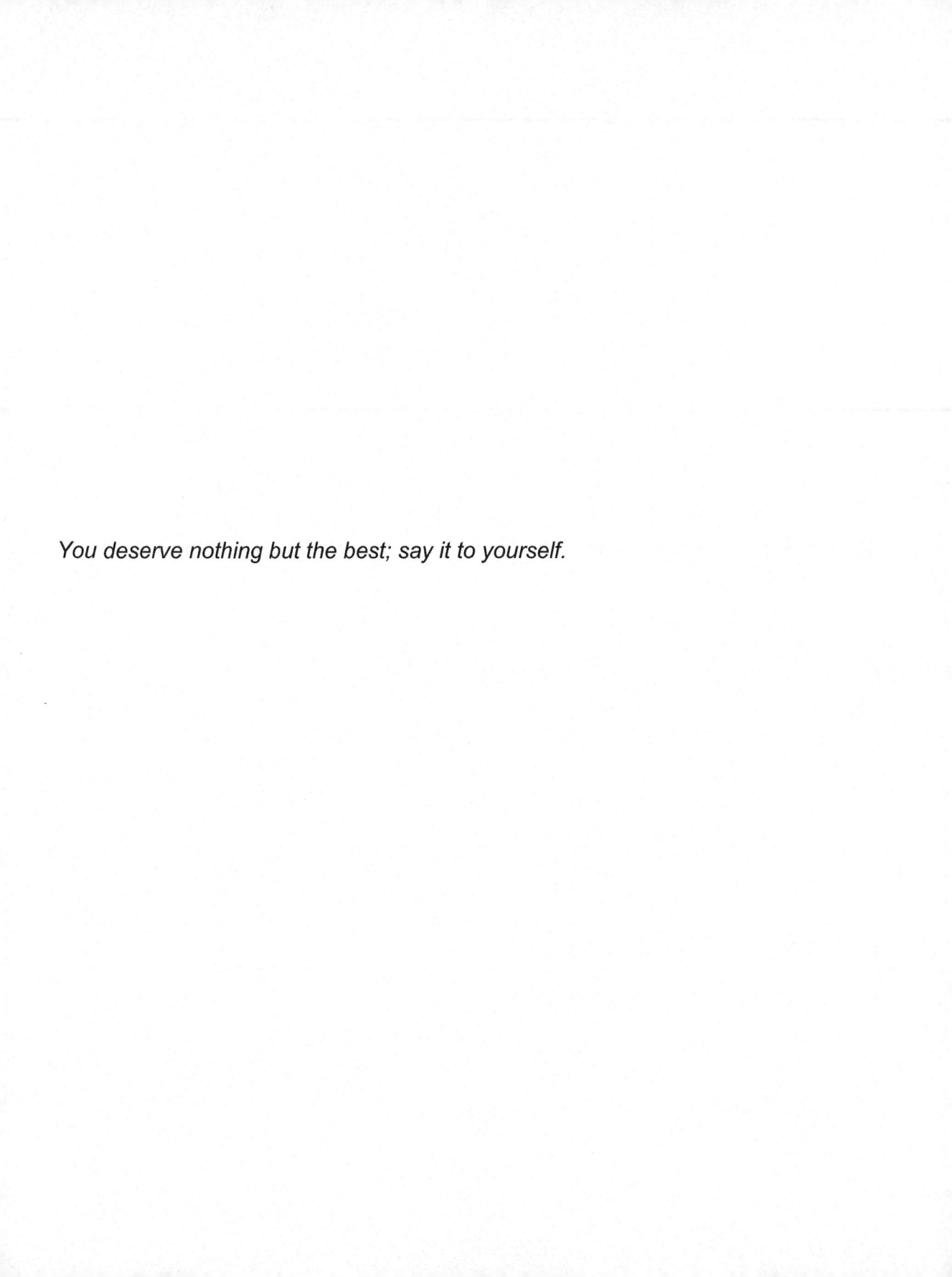

You deserve nothing but the best; say it to yourself.

We are all born with a purpose. Our biggest purpose is to focus on God.

Heaven is a place created for God. God wants us to make peace and teach the world on Earth about peace.

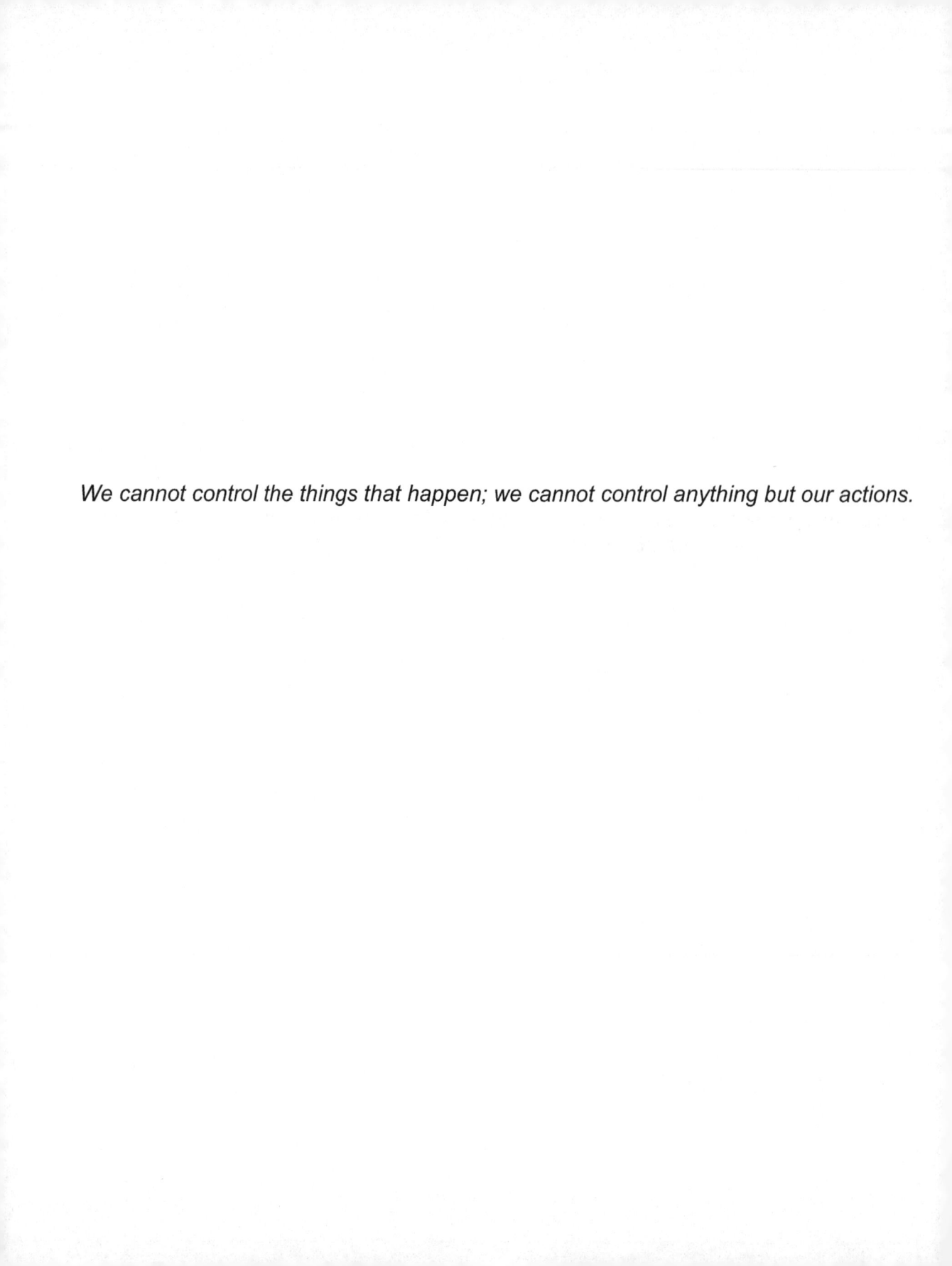

We cannot control the things that happen; we cannot control anything but our actions.

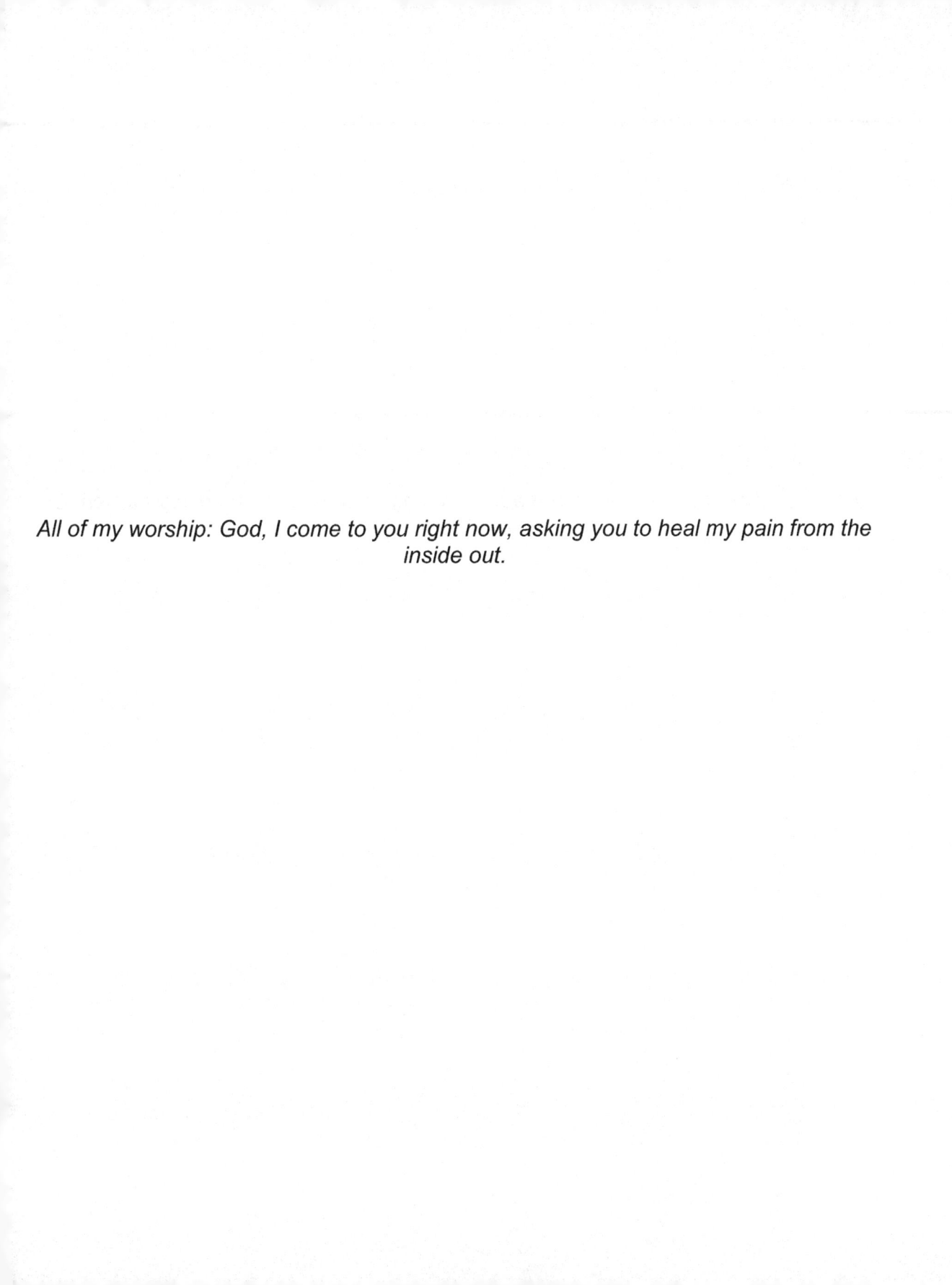

All of my worship: God, I come to you right now, asking you to heal my pain from the inside out.

I want to be free. I would like to be free. I'm letting go and releasing every burden. Clear my negative thoughts.

Allow me to be free in my mind; allow me to be free in my heart and walks of life.

God, I believe you're going to love me. You will hold me; you will love me. Not only that, but you'll set me free. You will set my soul on fire because I am free.

Touchy subject for me: The ones I love never love me back the way I desire them.

I truly don't think I will ever be loved the way I desire because my love is complicated.

When it comes to touch and feel, an expression, it takes time. But apart from that, I have learned to show love with materialistic things and be expressive in my words.

And then I found the direction of letting God guide me when it comes to people and their emotions and love.

Because I am so sensitive, I want to be very gentle with others' emotions and how I treat them when it comes to love.

God's love and word is unlike any other word!

God is in your fingertips.

Be You.

The healing journal never stops.

Keep shining bright and spreading positivity!

It's a struggle to see the light shine every day. It's very hard, especially when your light is dim and your mind is clouded by the things that surround you daily. The struggle begins when you open your eyes; doubt slowly creeps into your mind. The soul, the flesh, and the spirit are all fighting each other to rule your mind.

But the moment you identify with Christ, your mind instantly becomes calm and very aware because you have allowed the spirit to rule your mind. The soul and the flesh are constantly trying to interrupt your good thoughts. When you start to feel overwhelmed, overanalyze everything, and look at the sink, the problem, your mind says there's a certain way, there's a proper time in everything you do.

The soul displays all the stuff you are going through every day. The soul wants to get you off balance with unwanted problems. Then your flesh starts to get aggravated and steps out of the will of God. Your light is shaded because your mind is surrounded by negative thoughts. So, your mind questions, 'What light are you talking about when I can't feel or see God moving in my situation?'

Your energy is the light within you. You are not alone; you are light. The key is within you; His presence is forever with you. He lives in you. Let Him fight every problem outside, let Him stand in the gap for you, and let His light shine so bright within you that the shadow is His reflection that is in you.

You are loved, you are someone, and you are special. God created you for His greatness. Never forget that.

Continue to surround yourself with those who reciprocate the love you desire, not just blood. It's agape love.

Stay strong! Remember, there are people depending on you. Don't let past emotions and challenges affect your present. Walk with your head up, trusting God, and thanking Him for what He has done and will do. He will fulfill every promise, and with God as your comforter, you can overcome any challenge.

You are not alone; love surrounds you. God has made us for a time like this. Embrace it as your healing season.

Acknowledgements

Thank you for always being such an inspiration, family, and friends. I hope this brings you so much joy that you're overwhelmed in peace. Know that I love you and that I care for you from deep within. There's no one on this earth like you all. Continue to prosper, continue to shine, continue to be the torch, continue to stand no matter what it looks like around you. Thank you for all the love.

About the Author

As an author sharing the profound journey of faith, I invite you to walk with me. I express gratitude to the Lord, my family, friends, therapist, and even strangers that turned into family – new additions to my life – for keeping me on track through the chapters of life. May my words resonate with the divine guidance that has shaped my steps and provided strength in times of weakness. On this side of heaven existence, I continue to stand, unwavering, no matter the circumstances. I want to share the joy and experiences along with the journey. I've had a lot of overflow and blessings, and God has given me overwhelming peace, as my steps are led by the constant and reassuring presence of the Lord. So, reassuring.

Accomplishments along the way
-Doctoral in Biblical Psychology
-Master's and Bachelor's in Theology and Religious Studies
-Teacher Assistant Diploma:
-Licensed Cosmetologist
-Licensed Christian Therapist
-Phlebotomy Technician Program Certificate:
-The Gospel Ministry 2020
-Marriage Officiant: Symbolizing the celebration of unions.
-Let's not forget Author
Thank you, Lord!

Made in the USA
Coppell, TX
02 July 2024